THE NEW TEMPLE SHAKESPEARE

Edited by M. R. Ridley, M.A.

TIMON OF ATHENS

by William Shakespeare

London: J. M.

N

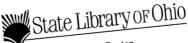

Editor's General Note

The Text. The editor has kept before him the aim of presenting to the modern reader the nearest possible approximation to what Shakespeare actually wrote. The text is therefore conservative, and is based on the earliest reliable printed text. But to avoid distraction (*a*) the spelling is modernised, and (*b*) a limited number of universally accepted emendations is admitted without comment. Where a Quarto text exists as well as the First Folio the passages which occur only in the Quarto are enclosed in square brackets [ ] and those which occur only in the Folio in brace brackets { }.

Scene Division. The rapid continuity of the Elizabethan curtainless production is lost by the 'traditional' scene divisions. Where there is an essential difference of place these scene divisions are retained. Where on the other hand the change of place is insignificant the scene division is indicated only by a space on the page. For ease of reference, however, the 'traditional' division is retained at the head of the page and in line numbering.

Notes. Passages on which there are notes are indicated by a † in the margin.

Punctuation adheres more closely than has been usual to the 'Elizabethan' punctuation of the early texts. It is often therefore more indicative of the way in which the lines were to be delivered than of their syntactical construction.

Glossaries are arranged on a somewhat novel principle, not alphabetically, but in the order in which the words or phrases occur. The editor is much indebted to Mr J. N. Bryson for his collaboration in the preparation of the glossaries.

Preface

The Text. The play was printed for the first time in the Folio of 1623. There is reason to suppose from the numbering of the pages that it took the place which had been originally intended for *Troilus and Cressida*. But whether there is any very real significance in this supposed substitution is more than doubtful. The text, if not ' the worst printed in the volume,' is certainly full of difficulties and at least apparent corruptions.

Date of Composition. For this there is no external evidence. Metrical tests place the play after *Hamlet*. The general tone of the play is that somewhat weary disillusionment, which yet has not the vigour to rise to tragedy, that one feels in *Troilus and Cressida*. And the author of it seems to have painfully in mind that problem of ingratitude which was in the mind of the author of *King Lear*.

The Authorship. The critics of this play have a sinister resemblance to the convocation of politic worms that set to work on the corpse of Polonius, though they are more eclectic in their tastes. They agree in one thing only, that the play is not the unaided or ungarbled or unmodified work of Shakespeare. Outside this general agreement, the permutations and combinations of the parts which are Shakespeare's, the parts which belong to an earlier play worked over by Shakespeare, the parts which he worked out in a rough draft and which were then completed by another hand, the parts which he never completed at all and had to be interpolated by another hand, the parts which are the result of an unskilful piecing together of actors' parts, and so on, and so on—their names are legion. All readers must feel reluctant to regard the play as we have it as a finished piece of Shakespeare's own work ; but the evidence for the various theories whereby we can legitimately escape from the repugnant conclusion is much too extensive and too intricate to be given here in full, and it cannot be effectively summarised. Readers must be referred to (*e.g.*) Mr K. Deighton's introduction to the 'Arden' edition of the play, where the evidence, such as it is, is very adequately presented by a refreshingly conservative editor, and in which a tribute, I think well justified, is paid to Verplanck. For the rest, there seems nothing to be done, for the purposes of this edition, but to give the play substantially as it appears in the First Folio ; that is, in the shape in which, when all is said and done, Heminge and Condell chose to give it to the world as the work of their friend, with all its imperfections on its head.

Sources of the Plot. In North's Plutarch, in the life of Antonius, there is a short account of Timon. Shakespeare could also have drawn upon Paynter's *Palace of Pleasure*, and, very particularly, if he could have arrived at it through the medium of a translation which does not appear to have existed, upon Lucian's dialogue, *Timon or the Misanthrope*. The apparent connection in many points between the play and the dialogue does strongly suggest that either Shakespeare had more Greek than he has been credited with, or that he was working over the production of an author who had read Lucian. It may be noticed that Timon had been in Shakespeare's mind as early as *L. L. L.*

Criticism. *Timon* is a savage play. There is an unrelieved bitterness about it unique in Shakespeare's work. It seems the work of a man not only preoccupied with the topic of ingratitude, as was perhaps the writer of *King Lear*, but also utterly disillusioned. With the exception of Flavius and Timon's servants there is not a character in it who does not merit Timon's disgust. If the world is made up of people like Timon's friends, like Alcibiades and his two whores, and like the professionally cynical Apemantus, if it is a world in which even the page catches the infection of the general rottenness, then we feel that we might as well become misanthropoi like Timon and hate mankind. One feels behind it something of that weary disgust with which Swift drew the Yahoos.

Hazlitt.[1]—Timon of Athens always appeared to us to be written with as intense a feeling of his subject as any one play of Shakespear. It is one of the few in which he seems to be in earnest throughout, never to trifle nor go out of his way. He does not relax in his efforts, nor lose sight of the unity of his design. It is the only play of our author in which spleen is the predominant feeling of the mind. It is as much a satire as a play : and contains some of the finest pieces of invective possible to be conceived, both in the snarling captious answers of the cynic Apemantus, and in the impassioned and more terrible imprecations of Timon. The latter remind the classical reader of the force and swelling impetuosity of the moral declamations in *Juvenal*, while the former have all the keenness and caustic severity of the old Stoic philosophers. The soul of Diogenes appears to have been seated on the lips of Apemantus. The churlish profession of misanthropy in the cynic is contrasted with the profound feeling of it in Timon, and also with the soldier-like and determined resentment of Alcibiades against his countrymen, who have banished him.

[1] *Characters of Shakespear's Plays.*

Dowden.[1]—It would seem that about this period Shakspere's mind was much occupied with the questions, In what temper are we to receive the injuries inflicted upon us by our fellow men? How are we to bear ourselves towards those that wrong us? How shall we secure our inward being from chaos amid the evils of the world? How shall we attain to the most just and noble attitude of soul in which life and the injuries of life may be confronted? Now, here, in Timon we see one way in which a man may make his response to the injuries of life; he may turn upon the world with a fruitless and suicidal rage. Shakspere was interested in the history of Timon, not merely as a dramatic study, and not merely for the sake of moral edification, but because he recognised in the Athenian misanthrope one whom he had known, an intimate acquaintance, the Timon of Shakspere's own breast. Shall we hesitate to admit that there was such a Timon in the breast of Shakspere? We are accustomed to speak of Shakspere's gentleness and Shakspere's tolerance so foolishly, that we find it easier to conceive of Shakspere as indulgent towards baseness and wickedness, than as feeling measureless rage and indignation against them —rage and indignation which would sometimes flash beyond their bounds, and strike at the whole wicked race of man. And it is certain that Shakspere's delight in human character, his quick and penetrating sympathy with almost every variety of man, saved him from any persistent injustice towards the world. But it can hardly be doubted, that the creator of Hamlet, of Lear, of Timon, saw clearly, and felt deeply, that there is a darker side to the world and to the soul of man.

[1] Quoted from *Shakspere: His Mind and Art* by permission of the Publishers, Messrs Kegan Paul, Trench, Trubner & Co., Ltd.

THE LIFE OF
TIMON OF ATHENS

DRAMATIS PERSONÆ

TIMON, *a noble Athenian.*

LUCIUS,
LUCULLUS, } *flattering lords.*
SEMPRONIUS,

VENTIDIUS, *one of Timon's false friends.*

ALCIBIADES, *an Athenian captain.*

APEMANTUS, *a churlish philosopher.*

FLAVIUS, *steward to Timon.*

Poet, Painter, Jeweller, and Merchant.

An old Athenian.

FLAMINIUS,
LUCILIUS, } *servants to Timon.*
SERVILIUS,

CAPHIS,
PHILOTUS,
TITUS, } *servants to Timon's creditors and to the Lords.*
HORTENSIUS,
And others,

A Page. A Fool. Three Strangers.

PHRYNIA,
TIMANDRA, } *mistresses to Alcibiades.*

Cupid and Amazons in the mask.

Other Lords, Senators, Officers, Banditti, and Attendants.

SCENE : *Athens, and the neighbouring woods.*

THE LIFE OF
TIMON OF ATHENS

Act First

SCENES I AND II

Athens.   A hall in Timon's house

*Enter Poet, Painter, Jeweller, Merchant, and others,
at several doors*

Po. Good day, sir.

Pai.   I am glad you're well.

Po. I have not seen you long ; how goes the world ?

Pai. It wears, sir, as it grows.

Po.   Ay, that's well known :
But what particular rarity ? what strange,
Which manifold record not matches ?   See,
Magic of bounty, all these spirits thy power
Hath conjur'd to attend.   I know the merchant.

Pai. I know them both : th' other's a jeweller.

Mer. O, 'tis a worthy lord !

Jew.   Nay, that's most fix'd.

Mer. A most incomparable man, breath'd, as it were,   10

To an untirable and continuate goodness :
He passes.

Jew. I have a jewel here—

Mer. O, pray, let's see't.   For the Lord Timon, sir?

Jew. If he will touch the estimate.   But for that—

Po. (*reciting to himself*) 'When we for recompense have
        praised the vile,
It stains the glory in that happy verse,
Which aptly sings the good.'

Mer. (*looking on the iewel*) 'Tis a good form.

Jew. And rich : here is a water, look ye.

Pai. You are rapt, sir, in some work, some dedication   20
To the great lord.

Po.   A thing slipp'd idly from me.
Our poesy is as a gum, which oozes
From whence 'tis nourish'd : the fire i' the flint
Shows not, till it be struck : our gentle flame
Provokes itself, and, like the current, flies
Each bound it chafes.   What have you there?

Pai. A picture, sir : when comes your book forth?

Po. Upon the heels of my presentment, sir.
Let's see your piece.

Pai. 'Tis a good piece.   30

Po. So 'tis, this comes off well, and excellent.

Pai. Indifferent.

o.   Admirable : how this grace
      Speaks his own standing ! what a mental power
      This eye shoots forth ! how big imagination
      Moves in this lip, to the dumbness of the gesture,
      One might interpret.

Pai. It is a pretty mocking of the life :
      Here is a touch : is 't good ?

Po.   I will say of it,
      It tutors nature, artificial strife
      Lives in these touches, livelier than life.   40
                    Enter certain Senators, and pass over

Pai. How this lord is follow'd !

Po. The senators of Athens, happy men !

Pai. Look, moe !

Po. You see this confluence, this great flood of visitors,
      I have, in this rough work, shap'd out a man
      Whom this beneath world doth embrace and hug
      With amplest entertainment : my free drift
      Halts not particularly, but moves itself
      In a wide sea of wax, no levell'd malice   †
      Infects one comma in the course I hold,   50
      But flies an eagle flight, bold, and forth on,
      Leaving no tract behind.

Pai. How shall I understand you ?

Po.   I will unbolt to you.

You see how all conditions, how all minds,
As well of glib and slippery creatures as
Of grave and austere quality, tender down
Their services to Lord Timon : his large fortune,
Upon his good and gracious nature hanging,
Subdues and properties to his love and tendance
All sorts of hearts ; yea, from the glass-fac'd flatterer 60
To Apemantus, that few things loves better
Than to abhor himself ; even he drops down
The knee before him, and returns in peace
Most rich in Timon's nod.

Pai.   I saw them speak together.

Po. Sir, I have upon a high and pleasant hill
Feign'd Fortune to be thron'd : the base o' the mount
Is rank'd with all deserts, all kind of natures
That labour on the bosom of this sphere,
To propagate their states ; amongst them all,
Whose eyes are on this sovereign lady fix'd,   70
One do I personate of Lord Timon's frame,
Whom Fortune with her ivory hand wafts to her,
Whose present grace to present slaves and servants
Translates his rivals.

Pai.   'Tis conceiv'd to scope.
This throne, this Fortune, and this hill, methinks,
With one man beckon'd from the rest below,

4

Bowing his head against the steepy mount
To climb his happiness, would be well express'd
In our condition

Po.　　　　　Ay, sir, but hear me on :
All those which were his fellows but of late,　　　80
Some better than his value, on the moment
Follow his strides, his lobbies fill with tendance,
Rain sacrificial whisperings in his ear,
Make sacred even his stirrup, and through him
Drink the free air.

Pai.　　　　　Ay, marry, what of these !

Po. When Fortune in her shift and change of mood
Spurns down her late belov'd, all his dependants
Which labour'd after him to the mountain's top
Even on their knees and hands, let him sit down,　†
Not one accompanying his declining foot.　　　90

Pai. 'Tis common :
A thousand moral paintings I can show,
That shall demonstrate these quick blows of Fortune's,
More pregnantly than words.　Yet you do well,
To show Lord Timon that mean eyes have seen
The foot above the head.

Trumpets sound.　Enter Lord Timon, addressing himself court-
eously to every suitor ; a Messenger from Ventidius talking
with him ; Lucilius and other servants following

Tim.   Imprison'd is he, say you?

Mes. Ay, my good lord, five talents is his debt;
    His means most short, his creditors most strait:
    Your honourable letter he desires
    To those have shut him up, which failing,   100
    Periods his comfort.

Tim.   Noble Ventidius, well:
    I am not of that feather to shake off
    My friend when he must need me. I do know him
    A gentleman that well deserves a help,
    Which he shall have. I'll pay the debt, and free him.

Mes. Your lordship ever binds him.

Tim. Commend me to him, I will send his ransom,
    And, being enfranchis'd, bid him come to me;
    'Tis not enough to help the feeble up,   110
    But to support him after. Fare you well.

Mes. All happiness to your honour!   *Exit*

Enter an old Athenian

Ath. Lord Timon, hear me speak.

Tim.   Freely, good father.

Ath. Thou hast a servant nam'd Lucilius.

Tim. I have so: what of him?

Ath. Most noble Timon, call the man before thee.

Tim. Attends he here, or no? Lucilius!

Luc. Here at your lordship's service.

6

Ath. This fellow here, Lord Timon, this thy creature,
By night frequents my house.   I am a man   120
That from my first have been inclin'd to thrift,
And my estate deserves an heir more rais'd
Than one which holds a trencher.

Tim.   Well: what further?

Ath. One only daughter have I, no kin else,
On whom I may confer what I have got:
The maid is fair, o' the youngest for a bride,
And I have bred her at my dearest cost
In qualities of the best.   This man of thine
Attempts her love: I prithee, noble lord,
Join with me to forbid him her resort,   130
Myself have spoke in vain.

Tim.   The man is honest.

Ath. Therefore he will be Timon,   †
His honesty rewards him in itself;
It must not bear my daughter.

Tim.   Does she love him?

Ath. She is young and apt:
Our own precedent passions do instruct us
What levity's in youth.

Tim. (to Lucilius)   Love you the maid?

Luc. Ay, my good lord, and she accepts of it.

Ath. If in her marriage my consent be missing,

7

I call the gods to witness, I will choose   140
  Mine heir from forth the beggars of the world,
  And dispossess her all.

Tim.   How shall she be endow'd
  If she be mated with an equal husband?

Ath. Three talents on the present; in future, all.

Tim. This gentleman of mine hath serv'd me long:
  To build his fortune, I will strain a little,
  For 'tis a bond in men. Give him thy daughter,
  What you bestow, in him I'll counterpoise,
  And make him weigh with her.

Ath.   Most noble lord,
  Pawn me to this your honour, she is his.   150

Tim. My hand to thee, mine honour on my promise.

Luc. Humbly I thank your lordship: never may
  That state or fortune fall into my keeping,
  Which is not ow'd to you!

                  Exeunt Lucilius and Old Athenian

Po. Vouchsafe my labour, and long live your lordship!

Tim. I thank you, you shall hear from me anon:
  Go not away. What have you there, my friend?

Pai. A piece of painting, which I do beseech
  Your lordship to accept.

Tim.   Painting is welcome.
  The painting is almost the natural man;   160

For since dishonour traffics with man's nature,
He is but outside: these pencill'd figures are
Even such as they give out.   I like your work,
And you shall find I like it; wait attendance
Till you hear further from me.

Pai.   The gods preserve ye!

Tim. Well fare you, gentleman: give me your hand.
We must needs dine together: sir, your jewel
Hath suffer'd under praise.

Jew.   What, my lord, dispraise?

Tim. A mere satiety of commendations.
If I should pay you for 't as 'tis extoll'd,   170
It would unclew me quite.

Jew.   My lord, 'tis rated
As those which sell would give: but you well know,
Things of like value, differing in the owners,
Are prized by their masters.   Believe 't, dear lord,
You mend the jewel by the wearing it.

Tim. Well mock'd.

Mer. No, my good lord, he speaks the common tongue,
Which all men speak with him.

Tim. Look who comes here, will you be chid?

                    Enter Apemantus

Jew. We'll bear with your lordship.

Mer.   He'll spare none.   180

Tim. Good morrow to thee, gentle Apemantus!

Ape. Till I be gentle, stay thou for thy good morrow.
When thou art Timon's dog, and these knaves honest.

Tim. Why dost thou call them knaves? thou know'st them not.

Ape. Are they not Athenians?

Tim. Yes.

Ape. Then I repent not.

Jew. You know me, Apemantus?

Ape. Thou know'st I do, I call'd thee by thy name.

Tim. Thou art proud, Apemantus?   190

Ape. Of nothing so much as that I am not like Timon.

Tim. Whither art going?

Ape. To knock out an honest Athenian's brains.

Tim. That 's a deed thou 'lt die for.

Ape. Right, if doing nothing be death by the law.

Tim. How lik'st thou this picture, Apemantus?

Ape. The best, for the innocence.

Tim. Wrought he not well that painted it?

Ape. He wrought better that made the painter, and yet
he 's but a filthy piece of work.   200

Pai. You 're a dog.

Ape. Thy mother 's of my generation: what 's she, if I
be a dog?

Tim. Wilt dine with me, Apemantus?

Ape. No: I eat not lords.

Tim. An thou shouldst, thou 'ldst anger ladies.

Ape. O, they eat lords ; so they come by great bellies.

Tim. That 's a lascivious apprehension.

Ape. So, thou apprehend'st it, take it for thy labour.

Tim. How dost thou like this jewel, Apemantus ?   210

Ape. Not so well as plain-dealing, which will not cost a
  man a doit.

Tim. What dost thou think 'tis worth ?

Ape. Not worth my thinking. How now, poet ?

Po. How now, philosopher ?

Ape. Thou liest.

Po. Art not one ?

Ape. Yes.

Po. Then I lie not.

Ape. Art not a poet ?   220

Po. Yes.

Ape. Then thou liest : look in thy last work, where thou
  hast feign'd him a worthy fellow.

Po. That 's not feign'd, he is so.

Ape. Yes, he is worthy of thee, and to pay thee for thy
  labour. He that loves to be flatter'd is worthy o'
  the flatterer. Heavens, that I were a lord !

Tim. What wouldst do then, Apemantus ?

Ape. E'en as Apemantus does now, hate a lord with my
  heart.   230

Tim. What, thyself?

Ape. Ay.

Tim. Wherefore?

Ape. That I had no angry wit to be a lord. Art not thou †
a merchant?

Mer. Ay, Apemantus.

Ape. Traffic confound thee, if the gods will not!

Mer. If traffic do it, the gods do it.

Ape. Traffic's thy god, and thy god confound thee!

> *Trumpet sounds. Enter a Messenger*

Tim. What trumpet's that? 240

Mes. 'Tis Alcibiades, and some twenty horse
All of companionship.

Tim. Pray entertain them, give them guide to us.

> *Exeunt some Attendants*

You must needs dine with me: go not you hence
Till I have thank'd you: when dinner's done,
Show me this piece. I am joyful of your sights.

> *Enter Alcibiades, with the rest*

Most welcome, sir!

Ape. So, so, there!

Aches contract and starve your supple joints!
That there should be small love 'mongst these sweet
knaves,
And all this courtesy! The strain of man's bred out 250

Into baboon and monkey.

Alc. Sir, you have sav'd my longing, and I feed
  Most hungerly on your sight.

Tim.   Right welcome, sir !
  Ere we depart, we 'll share a bounteous time
  In different pleasures.   Pray you, let us in.

                              Exeunt all but Apemantus
                    Enter two Lords

First Lord. What time o' day is 't, Apemantus ?

Ape. Time to be honest.

First Lord. That time serves still.

Ape. The most accursed thou, that still omitt'st it.

Sec. Lord. Thou art going to Lord Timon's feast ?   260

Ape. Ay, to see meat fill knaves, and wine heat fools.

Sec. Lord. Fare thee well, fare thee well.

Ape. Thou art a fool to bid me farewell twice.

Sec. Lord. Why, Apemantus ?

Ape. Shouldst have kept one to thyself, for I mean to give
  thee none.

First Lord. Hang thyself !

Ape. No, I will do nothing at thy bidding : make thy
  requests to thy friend.

Sec. Lord. Away, unpeaceable dog, or I 'll spurn thee   270
  hence !

Ape. I will fly, like a dog, the heels o' the ass.   *Exit*

First Lord. He's opposite to humanity. Come, shall **we in,**
    And taste Lord Timon's bounty? he outgoes
    The very heart of kindness.

Sec. Lord. He pours it out: Plutus, the god of gold,
    Is but his steward: no meed but he repays
    Sevenfold above itself: no gift to him,
    But breeds the giver a return, exceeding
    All use of quittance.

First Lord.   The noblest mind he carries   280
    That ever govern'd man.

Sec. Lord. Long may he live in fortunes! Shall we in?
    I'll keep you company.   *Exeunt*

*Hautboys playing loud music. A great banquet served in;
    Flavius and others attending; and then enter Lord Timon,
    Alcibiades, Lords, Senators, and Ventidius. Then comes,
    dropping after all, Apemantus, discontentedly, like himself.*

Ven. Most honour'd Timon,
    It hath pleas'd the gods to remember my father's age,
    And call him to long peace:
    He is gone happy, and has left me rich:
    Then, as in grateful virtue I am bound

To your free heart, I do return those talents,
Doubled with thanks and service, from whose help
I deriv'd liberty.

Tim.　　　　　　O, by no means,
Honest Ventidius ; you mistake my love,
I gave it freely ever, and there 's none　　　　　　**10**
Can truly say he gives, if he receives :
If our betters play at that game, we must not dare
To imitate them ; faults that are rich are fair.

Ven. A noble spirit !

Tim. Nay, my lords, ceremony was but devis'd at first
To set a gloss on faint deeds, hollow welcomes,
Recanting goodness, sorry ere 'tis shown :
But where there is true friendship, there needs none.
Pray, sit ; more welcome are ye to my fortunes
Than my fortunes to me.　　　　　　*They sit*　**20**

First Lord. My lord, we always have confess'd it.

Ape. Ho, ho, confess'd it ? hang'd it, have you not ?

Tim. O, Apemantus, you are welcome.

Ape.　　　　　　No :
You shall not make me welcome :
I come to have thee thrust me out of doors.

Tim. Fie, thou 'rt a churl, ye 've got a humour there
Does not become a man ; 'tis much to blame.
They say, my lords, ' *ira furor brevis est* ; ' but yond

15

man is ever angry.   Go, let him have a table by himself; for he does neither affect company, nor is he   30
fit for 't indeed.

Ape. Let me stay at thine apperil, Timon:
I come to observe; I give thee warning on 't.

Tim. I take no heed of thee: thou 'rt an Athenian,
therefore welcome: I myself would have no power,
prithee, let my meat make thee silent.

Ape. I scorn thy meat, 'twould choke me: for I should
ne'er flatter thee.   O you gods, what a number of
men eats Timon, and he sees 'em not! It grieves
me to see so many dip their meat in one man's blood,   40
and all the madness is, he cheers them up too.
I wonder men dare trust themselves with men:
Methinks they should invite them without knives,
Good for their meat, and safer for their lives.
There 's much example for 't; the fellow that sits
next him, now parts bread with him, pledges the
breath of him in a divided draught, is the readiest
man to kill him: 't has been prov'd.   If I were a
huge man, I should fear to drink at meals.
Lest they should spy my windpipe's dangerous notes: †
Great men should drink with harness on their throats.

Tim. My lord, in heart; and let the health go round.   52
Sec. Lord. Let it flow this way, my good lord.

Ape. Flow this way? A brave fellow! he keeps his
tides well; those healths will make thee and thy
state look ill, Timon. Here's that which is too weak
to be a sinner, honest water, which ne'er left man
i' the mire:
This and my food are equals; there's no odds:
Feasts are too proud to give thanks to the gods.   60

Apemantus's Grace

Immortal gods, I crave no pelf,
I pray for no man but myself,
Grant I may never prove so fond,
To trust man on his oath or bond:
Or a harlot for her weeping,
Or a dog that seems a-sleeping,
Or a keeper with my freedom,
Or my friends, if I should need 'em.
Amen. So fall to't:
Rich men sin, and I eat root.   70

Eats and drinks

Much good dich thy good heart, Apemantus!

Tim. Captain Alcibiades, your heart's in the field now.

Alc. My heart is ever at your service, my lord.

Tim. You had rather be at a breakfast of enemies than a
dinner of friends.

Alc. So they were bleeding-new, my lord, there's no meat

17

like 'em; I could wish my best friend at such a feast.

Ape. Would all those flatterers were thine enemies, then, that then thou mightst kill 'em; and bid me to 'em! 80

First Lord. Might we but have that happiness, my lord, that you would once use our hearts, whereby we might express some part of our zeals, we should think ourselves for ever perfect.

Tim. O, no doubt, my good friends, but the gods themselves have provided that I shall have much help from you: how had you been my friends else? why have you that charitable title from thousands? Did not you chiefly belong to my heart? I have told more of you to myself than you can with modesty 90 speak in your own behalf. And thus far I confirm you. O you gods (think I) what need we have any friends, if we should ne'er have need of 'em? they were the most needless creatures living, should we ne'er have use for 'em; and would most resemble sweet instruments hung up in cases, that keeps their sounds to themselves. Why, I have often wished myself poorer, that I might come nearer to you. We are born to do benefits: and what better or properer can we call our own than the riches of our friends? 100 O, what a precious comfort 'tis, to have so many

like brothers commanding one another's fortunes!
O joy's e'en made away ere 't can be born! Mine
eyes cannot hold out water, methinks: to forget
their faults, I drink to you.

Ape. Thou weep'st to make them drink, Timon.

ec. Lord. Joy had the like conception in our eyes,
And at that instant like a babe sprung up.

Ape. Ho, ho! I laugh to think that babe a bastard.

Third Lord. I promise you, my lord, you mov'd me much. 110

Ape. Much!   *Tucket, within*

Tim. What means that trump?

Enter a Servant

How now?

Serv. Please you, my lord, there are certain ladies most
desirous of admittance.

Tim. Ladies? what are their wills?

Serv. There comes with them a forerunner, my lord,
which bears that office, to signify their pleasures.

Tim. I pray, let them be admitted.

Enter Cupid

Cup. Hail to thee, worthy Timon, and to all
That of his bounties taste! The five best senses   120
Acknowledge thee their patron, and come freely
To gratulate thy plenteous bosom:
Th' ear, taste, touch, smell, pleas'd from thy table rise;

19

They only now come but to feast thine eyes.

Tim. They're welcome all, let 'em have kind admittance.
Music make their welcome !   *Exit Cupid*

First Lord. You see, my lord, how ample you're belov'd.

*Music. Re-enter Cupid, with a mask of Ladies as Amazons,
with lutes in their hands, dancing and playing*

Ape. Hoy-day, what a sweep of vanity comes this way !
They dance ! they are mad women.
Like madness is the glory of this life,   †
As this pomp shows to a little oil and root.   13?
We make ourselves fools, to disport ourselves,
And spend our flatteries, to drink those men
Upon whose age we void it up again
With poisonous spite and envy.
Who lives, that's not depraved or depraves ?
Who dies, that bears not one spurn to their graves
Of their friends' gift ?
I should fear, those that dance before me now
Would one day stamp upon me : 't has been done ; 140
Men shut their doors against a setting sun.

*The Lords rise from table, with much adoring of Timon and
to show their loves, each singles out an Amazon, and all
dance, men with women, a lofty strain or two to the
hautboys, and cease*

Tim. You have done our pleasures much grace, fair ladies,

Set a fair fashion on our entertainment,
Which was not half so beautiful and kind :
You have added worth unto 't, and lustre,
And entertain'd me with mine own device.
I am to thank you for 't.

First Lady. My lord, you take us even at the best.

Ape. Faith, for the worst is filthy, and would not hold
    taking, I doubt me.   150

Tim. Ladies, there is an idle banquet attends you,
    Please you to dispose yourselves.

All Lad. Most thankfully, my lord.

                        Exeunt Cupid and Ladies

Tim. Flavius !

Fla. My lord ?

Tim.   The little casket bring me hither.

Fla. Yes, my lord. *(aside)* More jewels yet ?
    There is no crossing him in 's humour,
    Else I should tell him well, i' faith I should ;
    When all 's spent, he 'ld be cross'd then, an he could :
    'Tis pity bounty had not eyes behind,   160
    That man might ne'er be wretched for his mind.

                                Exit

First Lord. Where be our men ?

Serv. Here, my lord, in readiness.

Sec. Lord. Our horses !

Re-enter Flavius, with the casket

Tim. O my friends,
    I have one word to say to you : look you, my good
        lord,
    I must entreat you honour me so much
    As to advance this jewel, accept it, and wear it,
    Kind my lord.

First Lord. I am so far already in your gifts,—   170

All. So are we all.

Enter a Servant

Serv. My lord, there are certain nobles of the senate
    newly alighted, and come to visit you.

Tim. They are fairly welcome.

Fla. I beseech your honour, vouchsafe me a word ; it
    does concern you near.

Tim. Near ? why then another time I 'll hear thee.
    I prithee, let 's be provided to show them entertain-
    ment.

Fla. (*aside*) I scarce know how.

Enter another Servant

Sec. Serv. May it please your honour, Lord Lucius   180
    (Out of his free love) hath presented to you
    Four milk-white horses, trapp'd in silver.

Tim. I shall accept them fairly : let the presents
    Be worthily entertain'd.

Enter a third Servant

How now ? what news ?

Third Serv. Please you, my lord, that honourable gentleman, Lord Lucullus, entreats your company to-
morrow, to hunt with him, and has sent your honour
two brace of greyhounds.

Tim. I 'll hunt with him, and let them be receiv'd,
Not without fair reward.

Fla.   *(aside)* What will this come to ?   190
He commands us to provide, and give great gifts,
and all out of an empty coffer :
Nor will he know his purse, or yield me this,
To show him what a beggar his heart is,
Being of no power to make his wishes good.
His promises fly so beyond his state,
That what he speaks is all in debt, he owes
For every word ; he is so kind that he now
Pays interest for 't ; his land 's put to their books.
Well, would I were gently put out of office,   200
Before I were forc'd out !
Happier is he that has no friend to feed,
Than such that do e'en enemies exceed.
I bleed inwardly for my lord.   *Exit*

Tim.   You do yourselves
Much wrong, you bate too much of your own merits.

Here, my lord, a trifle of our love.

Sec. Lord. With more than common thanks I will receive it.

Third Lord. O, he 's the very soul of bounty !

Tim. And now I remember, my lord, you gave good
    words the other day of a bay courser I rode on. 210
    'Tis yours because you lik'd it.

Third Lord. O, I beseech you, pardon me, my lord, in that.

Tim. You may take my word, my lord ; I know no man
    Can justly praise but what he does affect :
    I weigh my friend's affection with mine own :
    I 'll tell you true.   I 'll call to you.

All Lords. O, none so welcome.

Tim. I take all and your several visitations
    So kind to heart, 'tis not enough to give :
    Methinks, I could deal kingdoms to my friends,   220
    And ne'er be weary.   Alcibiades,
    Thou art a soldier, therefore seldom rich,
    It comes in charity to thee : for all thy living
    Is 'mongst the dead ; and all the lands thou hast
    Lie in a pitch'd field.

Alc. Ay, defil'd land, my lord.

First Lord. We are so virtuously bound—

Tim.   And so
    Am I to you.

Sec. Lord. So infinitely endear'd—

Tim. All to you.   Lights, more lights !   230
First Lord. The best of happiness,
    Honour, and fortunes, keep with you, Lord Timon !
Tim. Ready for his friends.

                    Exeunt all but Apemantus and Timon
Ape.   What a coil 's here !
    Serving of becks and jutting-out of bums !
    I doubt whether their legs be worth the sums
    That are given for 'em.   Friendship 's full of dregs :
    Methinks false hearts should never have sound legs.
    Thus honest fools lay out their wealth on court'sies.
Tim. Now, Apemantus (if thou wert not sullen)
    I would be good to thee.   240
Ape. No, I 'll nothing : for if I should be brib'd too, there
    would be none left to rail upon thee, and then thou
    wouldst sin the faster.   Thou giv'st so long, Timon (I
    fear me) thou wilt give away thyself in paper shortly. †
    What needs these feasts, pomps and vain-glories ?
Tim. Nay, an you begin to rail on society once, I am
    sworn not to give regard to you.   Farewell, and
    come with better music.   *Exit*
Ape. So : thou wilt not hear me now, thou shalt not   250
    then.   I 'll lock thy heaven from thee :
    O, that men's ears should be
    To counsel deaf, but not to flattery !   *Exit*

Act Second

SCENE I

A Senator's house

Enter a Senator, with papers in his hand

Sen. And late five thousand : to Varro and to Isidore
    He owes nine thousand, besides my former sum,
    Which makes it five and twenty.   Still in motion
    Of raging waste ?   It cannot hold, it will not.
    If I want gold, steal but a beggar's dog
    And give it Timon, why, the dog coins gold.
    If I would sell my horse, and buy twenty moe
    Better than he, why, give my horse to Timon ;
    Ask nothing, give it him, it foals me straight
    And able horses : no porter at his gate,   † 10
    But rather one that smiles, and still invites
    All that pass by.   It cannot hold, no reason
    Can found his state in safety.   Caphis, ho !
    Caphis, I say !

                Enter Caphis

Cap.   Here, sir ; what is your pleasure ?

Sen. Get on your cloak, and haste you to Lord Timon,

Importune him for my moneys, be not ceas'd
With slight denial; nor then silenc'd, when—
' Commend me to your master '—and the cap
Plays in the right hand, thus : but tell him,
My uses cry to me ; I must serve my turn   20
Out of mine own, his days and times are past,
And my reliances on his fracted dates
Have smit my credit.   I love, and honour him,
But must not break my back to heal his finger.
Immediate are my needs, and my relief
Must not be toss'd and turn'd to me in words,
But find supply immediate.   Get you gone,
Put on a most importunate aspect,
A visage of demand ; for I do fear
When every feather sticks in his own wing,   30
Lord Timon will be left a naked gull,
Which flashes now a phœnix ; get you gone.

Cap. I go, sir.

Sen. Ay, go, sir !   Take the bonds along with you,
And have the dates in.   Come.

Cap.   I will, sir.

Sen.   Go.   *Exeunt*

SCENE II

A hall in Timon's house

Enter Flavius, with many bills in his hand

Fla. No care, no stop, so senseless of expense,
    That he will neither know how to maintain it,
    Nor cease his flow of riot.   Takes no account
    How things go from him, nor resumes no care
    Of what is to continue : never mind
    Was to be so unwise, to be so kind.
    What shall be done, he will not hear, till feel :
    I must be round with him, now he comes from
       hunting.
    Fie, fie, fie, fie !

    Enter Caphis, with the Servants of Isidore and Varro

Cap. Good even, Varro : what, you come for money ?   **10**

Var. Serv. Is 't not your business too ?

Cap. It is, and yours too, Isidore ?

Isid. Serv. It is so.

Cap. Would we were all discharg'd !

Var. Serv. I fear it.

Cap. Here comes the lord.

    Enter Timon, Alcibiades, Lords, and others

Tim. So soon as dinner 's done, we 'll forth again,

My Alcibiades. With me? what is your will?

Cap. My lord, here is a note of certain dues.

Tim. Dues? Whence are you?

Cap.   Of Athens here, my lord.   20

Tim. Go to my steward.

Cap. Please it your lordship, he hath put me off
    To the succession of new days this month:
    My master is awak'd by great occasion
    To call upon his own, and humbly prays you
    That with your other noble parts you 'll suit,
    In giving him his right.

Tim.   Mine honest friend,
    I prithee but repair to me next morning.

Cap. Nay, good my lord,—

Tim.   Contain thyself, good friend.

Var. Serv. One Varro's servant, my good lord,—   30

Isid. Serv. From Isidore; he humbly prays your speedy
    payment.

Cap. If you did know, my lord, my master's wants,—

Var. Serv. 'Twas due on forfeiture, my lord, six weeks,
    and past.

Isid. Serv. Your steward puts me off, my lord, and I
    Am sent expressly to your lordship.

Tim. Give me breath.
    I do beseech you, good my lords, keep on,

I'll wait upon you instantly.

Exeunt Alcibiades, Lords, &c.

(*to Fla.*) Come hither: pray you, 40
How goes the world, that I am thus encounter'd
With clamorous demands of debt, broken bonds,
And the detention of long-since-due debts,
Against my honour?

Fla.   Please you, gentlemen,
The time is unagreeable to this business:
Your importunacy cease, till after dinner,
That I may make his lordship understand
Wherefore you are not paid.

Tim. Do so my friends; see them well entertain'd   *Exit*
Fla. Pray, draw near.   *Exit* 50

Enter Apemantus and Fool

Cap. Stay, stay, here comes the fool with Apemantus, let's
ha' some sport with 'em.

Var. Serv. Hang him, he'll abuse us.

Isid. Serv. A plague upon him, dog!

Var. Serv. How dost, fool?

Ape. Dost dialogue with thy shadow?

Var. Serv. I speak not to thee.

Ape. No, 'tis to thyself. (*to the Fool*) Come away.

Isid. Serv. There's the fool hangs on your back already.

Ape. No, thou stand'st single, thou 'rt not on him yet. 60

Cap. Where's the fool now?

Ape. He last ask'd the question. Poor rogues, and usurers' men, bawds between gold and want!

All Serv. What are we, Apemantus?

Ape. Asses.

All Serv. Why?

Ape. That you ask me what you are, and do not know yourselves. Speak to 'em, fool.

Fool. How do you, gentlemen?

All Serv. Gramercies, good fool: how does your mistress?   70

Fool. She's e'en setting on water to scald such chickens as you are. Would we could see you at Corinth!

Ape. Good! gramercy.

Enter Page

Fool. Look you, here comes my master's page.

Page (*to the Fool*) Why, how now, captain? what do you in this wise company? How dost thou, Apemantus?

Ape. Would I had a rod in my mouth, that I might answer thee profitably.

Page. Prithee, Apemantus, read me the superscription of these letters, I know not which is which.   80

Ape. Canst not read?

Page. No.

Ape. There will little learning die then, that day thou art hang'd. This is to Lord Timon, this to Alcibiades.

31

Go; thou wast born a bastard, and thou 'lt die a
bawd.

*Page.*Thou wast whelp'd a dog, and thou shalt famish a
dog's death. Answer not, I am gone.   *Exit*

*Ape.*E'en so thou outrun'st grace; fool, I will go with
you to Lord Timon's.   90

*Fool.*Will you leave me there?

*Ape.*If Timon stay at home. You three serve three
usurers?

All Serv. I would they serv'd us!

*Ape.*So would I,—as good a trick as ever hangman serv'd
thief.

*Fool.*Are you three usurers' men?

All Serv. Ay, fool.

*Fool.*I think no usurer but has a fool to his servant. My
mistress is one, and I am her fool: when men come   100
to borrow of your masters, they approach sadly, and
go away merry; but they enter my master's house
merrily, and go away sadly. The reason of this?

Var. Serv. I could render one.

*Ape.*Do it then, that we may account thee a whoremaster, and a knave, which notwithstanding thou
shalt be no less esteem'd.

Var. Serv. What is a whoremaster, fool?

*Fool.*A fool in good clothes, and something like thee.

'Tis a spirit, sometime 't appears like a lord, some- 110
time like a lawyer, sometime like a philosopher,
with two stones moe than 's artificial one. He is
very often like a knight ; and generally, in all shapes
that man goes up and down in, from fourscore to
thirteen, this spirit walks in.

Var. Serv. Thou art not altogether a fool.

Fool. Nor thou altogether a wise man ; as much foolery
as I have, so much wit thou lack'st.

Ape. That answer might have become Apemantus.

All Serv. Aside, aside, here comes Lord Timon.   120

    Re-enter Timon and Flavius

Ape. Come with me, fool, come.

Fool. I do not always follow lover, elder brother, and
woman ; sometime the philosopher.

       Exeunt Apemantus and Fool

Fla. Pray you, walk near, I 'll speak with you anon.

         Exeunt Servants

Tim. You make me marvel wherefore, ere this time,
 Had you not fully laid my state before me,
 That I might so have rated my expense
 As I had leave of means.

Fla.   You would not hear me
 At many leisures I propos'd.

Tim.   Go to :

Perchance some single vantages you took,   130
When my indisposition put you back,
And that unaptness made your minister,
Thus to excuse yourself.

Fla.   O my good lord,
At many times I brought in my accounts,
Laid them before you, you would throw them off,
And say, you found them in mine honesty;
When for some trifling present you have bid me
Return so much, I have shook my head, and wept:
Yea, 'gainst the authority of manners, pray'd you
To hold your hand more close: I did endure   140
Not seldom, nor no slight checks, when I have
Prompted you in the ebb of your estate,
And your great flow of debts; my lov'd lord,
Though you hear now (too late) yet now 's a time
The greatest of your having lacks a half
To pay your present debts.

Tim.   Let all my land be sold.

Fla. 'Tis all engag'd, some forfeited and gone,
And what remains will hardly stop the mouth
Of present dues; the future comes apace:
What shall defend the interim? and at length   150
How goes our reckoning?

Tim. To Lacedæmon did my land extend.

Fla. O my good lord, the world is but a word,
　　　Were it all yours, to give it in a breath,
　　　How quickly were it gone !

Tim.　　　　　　　　　　You tell me true.

Fla. If you suspect my husbandry or falsehood,
　　　Call me before the exactest auditors,
　　　And set me on the proof.   So the gods bless me,
　　　When all our offices have been oppress'd
　　　With riotous feeders, when our vaults have wept   160
　　　With drunken spilth of wine ; when every room
　　　Hath blaz'd with lights, and bray'd with mistrelsy,
　　　I have retir'd me to a wasteful cock,　　　　　†
　　　And set mine eyes at flow.

Tim.　　　　　　　　　　Prithee, no more.

Fla. Heavens, have I said, the bounty of this lord !
　　　How many prodigal bits have slaves and peasants
　　　This night englutted !   Who is not Timon's ?
　　　What heart, head, sword, force, means, but is Lord
　　　　　Timon's ?
　　　Great Timon, noble, worthy, royal Timon !
　　　Ah, when the means are gone, that buy this praise,   170
　　　The breath is gone whereof this praise is made :
　　　Feast-won, fast-lost ; one cloud of winter showers,
　　　These flies are couch'd.

Tim.　　　　　　　　　　Come, sermon me no further.

No villanous bounty yet hath pass'd my heart;
Unwisely, not ignobly, have I given.
Why dost thou weep, canst thou the conscience lack,
To think I shall lack friends? Secure thy heart;
If I would broach the vessels of my love,
And try the argument of hearts, by borrowing,
Men, and men's fortunes could I frankly use   180
As I can bid thee speak.

Fla.   Assurance bless your thoughts!

Tim. And in some sort these wants of mine are crown'd,
That I account them blessings. For by these
Shall I try friends. You shall perceive how you
Mistake my fortunes; I am wealthy in my friends.
Within there! Flaminius! Servilius!

Enter Flaminius, Servilius, and other Servants

Servants. My lord? my lord?

Tim. I will dispatch you severally. You to Lord Lucius,
to Lord Lucullus you, I hunted with his honour to-
day; you to Sempronius; commend me to their   190
loves; and I am proud, say, that my occasions have
found time to use 'em toward a supply of money:
let the request be fifty talents.

Flam. As you have said, my lord.

Fla. (aside) Lord Lucius and Lucullus? hum!

Tim. Go you, sir, to the senators—

Of whom, even to the state's best health, I have
Deserv'd this hearing—bid 'em send o' the instant
A thousand talents to me.

Fla.   I have been bold,
(For that I knew it the most general way)   200
To them, to use your signet and your name,
But they do shake their heads, and I am here
No richer in return.

Tim.   Is 't true ? can't be ?

Fla. They answer in a joint and corporate voice,
That now they are at fall, want treasure, cannot
Do what they would, are sorry : you are honourable,
But yet they could have wish'd—they know not—
Something hath been amiss ; a noble nature
May catch a wrench ; would all were well ; 'tis
        pity :—
And so, intending other serious matters,   210
After distasteful looks and these hard fractions,
With certain half-caps and cold-moving nods
They froze me into silence.

Tim.   You gods, reward them !
Prithee, man, look cheerly.   These old fellows
Have their ingratitude in them hereditary :
Their blood is cak'd, 'tis cold, it seldom flows,
'Tis lack of kindly warmth, they are not kind ;

'd   37

And nature, as it grows again toward earth,
Is fashion'd for the journey, dull and heavy.
(*To a Serv.*) Go to Ventidius.   (*to Fla.*) Prithee, be
    not sad;   220
Thou art true and honest; ingeniously I speak,
No blame belongs to thee.   (*to Serv.*) Ventidius lately
Buried his father, by whose death he's stepp'd
Into a great estate: when he was poor,
Imprison'd, and in scarcity of friends,
I clear'd him with five talents: greet him from me,
Bid him suppose some good necessity
Touches his friend, which craves to be remember'd
With those five talents.   (*exit Serv.*)   (*to Fla.*) That
    had, giv't these fellows
To whom 'tis instant due.   Ne'er speak, or think   230
That Timon's fortunes 'mong his friends can sink.

Fla. I would I could not think it: that thought is bounty's
    foe;
Being free itself, it thinks all others so.   *Exeunt*

Act Third

SCENES I, II, III

A room in Lucullus's house

Flaminius waiting.   Enter a Servant to him

Serv. I have told my lord of you, he is coming down to you.

Flam. I thank you, sir.

Enter Lucullus

Serv. Here's my lord.

Lucul. (*aside*) One of Lord Timon's men? a gift,
I warrant. Why, this hits right; I dreamt of a
silver basin and ewer to-night. Flaminius, honest
Flaminius, you are very respectively welcome, sir.
Fill me some wine. (*exit Servant.*) And how does
that honourable, complete, free-hearted gentleman of
Athens, thy very bountiful good lord and master?   10

Flam. His health is well, sir.

Lucul. I am right glad that his health is well, sir: and
what hast thou there under thy cloak, pretty
Flaminius?

Flam. Faith, nothing but an empty box, sir, which, in my
lord's behalf, I come to entreat your honour to

supply : who, having great and instant occasion to
use fifty talents, hath sent to your lordship to furnish him ; nothing doubting your present assistance
therein.   20

Lucul. La, la, la, la ! 'nothing doubting,' says he ? Alas,
good lord ! a noble gentleman 'tis, if he would not
keep so good a house. Many a time and often I
ha' dined with him, and told him on 't, and come
again to supper to him of purpose, to have him
spend less, and yet he would embrace no counsel,
take no warning by my coming ; every man has
his fault, and honesty is his. I ha' told him on 't,
but I could ne'er get him from 't.

Re-enter Servant, with wine

Serv. Please your lordship, here is the wine.   30

Lucul. Flaminius, I have noted thee always wise. Here 's
to thee.

Flam. Your lordship speaks your pleasure.

Lucul. I have observed thee always for a towardly prompt
spirit—give thee thy due—and one that knows
what belongs to reason ; and canst use the time
well, if the time use thee well. Good parts in thee
—(*to Serv.*) get you gone, sirrah. (*exit Serv.*)
Draw nearer, honest Flaminius. Thy lord's a
bountiful gentleman, but thou art wise, and thou   40

know'st well enough (although thou com'st to me)
that this is no time to lend money, especially upon
bare friendship without security.   Here's three
solidares for thee: good boy, wink at me, and say
thou saw'st me not.   Fare thee well.

Flam. Is't possible the world should so much differ,
   And we alive that liv'd?   Fly, damned baseness,   †
   To him that worships thee !

                              Throwing back the money

Lucul. Ha?   now I see thou art a fool, and fit for thy
   master.   *Exit*   50

Flam. May these add to the number that may scald thee !
   Let molten coin be thy damnation,
   Thou disease of a friend, and not himself :
   Has friendship such a faint and milky heart,
   It turns in less than two nights?   O you gods,
   I feel my master's passion.   This slave,
   Unto his honour, has my lord's meat in him :
   Why should it thrive, and turn to nutriment,
   When he is turn'd to poison?
   O, may diseases only work upon't :   60
   And, when he's sick to death, let not that part of
       nature
   Which my lord paid for, be of any power
   To expel sickness, but prolong his hour !   *Exit*

41

A public place

Enter Lucius, with three Strangers

Luc. Who, the Lord Timon? He is my very good
friend and an honourable gentleman.

First Stran. We know him for no less, though we are
but strangers to him. But I can tell you one
thing, my lord, and which I hear from common
rumours, now Lord Timon's happy hours are done
and past, and his estate shrinks from him.

Luc. Fie, no, do not believe it : he cannot want for money.

Sec. Stran. But believe you this, my lord, that not long
ago one of his men was with the Lord Lucullus to   10
borrow so many talents, nay, urg'd extremely for 't,
and showed what necessity belong'd to 't, and yet
was denied.

Luc. How?

Sec. Stran. I tell you, denied, my lord.

Luc. What a strange case was that ! now, before the
gods, I am asham'd on 't. Denied that honourable
man ? there was very little honour show'd in 't.
For my own part, I must needs confess, I have
received some small kindnesses from him, as money,   20

42

plate, jewels, and suchlike trifles; nothing com-
paring to his: yet, had he mistook him, and sent
to me, I should ne'er have denied his occasion so
many talents.

Enter Servilius

Ser. See, by good hap, yonder's my lord, I have sweat
to see his honour. My honour'd lord !

Luc. Servilius ? you are kindly met, sir. Fare thee well,
commend me to thy honourable virtuous lord, my
very exquisite friend.

Ser. May it please your honour, my lord hath sent— 30

Luc. Ha ? what has he sent ? I am so much endear'd to
that lord ; he's ever sending : how shall I thank
him, think'st thou ? And what has he sent now ?

Ser. Has only sent his present occasion now, my lord :
requesting your lordship to supply his instant use
with so many talents.

Luc. I know his lordship is but merry with me,
He cannot want fifty five hundred talents. †

Ser. But in the mean time he wants less, my lord.
If his occasion were not virtuous, 40
I should not urge it half so faithfully.

Luc. Dost thou speak seriously, Servilius ?

Ser. Upon my soul, 'tis true, sir.

Luc. What a wicked beast was I to disfurnish myself

43

against such a good time, when I might ha' shown
myself honourable! how unluckily it happened, that
I should purchase the day before for a little part,
and undo a great deal of honour! Servilius, now,
before the gods, I am not able to do—the more
beast, I say:—I was sending to use Lord Timon 50
myself, these gentlemen can witness; but I would
not for the wealth of Athens I had done 't now.
Commend me bountifully to his good lordship, and
I hope his honour will conceive the fairest of me,
because I have no power to be kind. And tell him
this from me, I count it one of my greatest afflictions,
say, that I cannot pleasure such an honourable
gentleman. Good Servilius, will you befriend me
so far as to use mine own words to him?

Ser. Yes, sir, I shall.   60

Luc. I 'll look you out a good turn, Servilius.

                                                            Exit Servilius

True, as you said, Timon is shrunk indeed,
And he that 's once denied will hardly speed.   *Exit*

First Stran. Do you observe this, Hostilius?

Sec. Stran.   Ay, too well.

First Stran. Why, this is the world's soul, and just of the
                same piece

   Is every flatterer's spirit: who can call him

44

His friend that dips in the same dish? for, in
My knowing, Timon has been this lord's father,
And kept his credit with his purse;
Supported his estate, nay, Timon's money   70
Has paid his men their wages.   He ne'er drinks,
But Timon's silver treads upon his lip,
And yet, O see the monstrousness of man,
When he looks out in an ungrateful shape,
He does deny him, in respect of his,
What charitable men afford to beggars.

Third Stran. Religion groans at it.

First Stran.   For mine own part,
I never tasted Timon in my life,
Nor came any of his bounties over me,
To mark me for his friend.   Yet, I protest,   80
For his right noble mind, illustrious virtue,
And honourable carriage,
Had his necessity made use of me,
I would have put my wealth into donation,
And the best half should have return'd to him,
So much I love his heart: but, I perceive,
Men must learn now with pity to dispense,
For policy sits above conscience.   *Exeunt*

A room in Sempronius' house

Enter Sempronius, and a Servant of Timon's

Sem. Must he needs trouble me in 't,—hum !—'above all
   others ?

  He might have tried Lord Lucius, or Lucullus,

  And now Ventidius is wealthy too,

  Whom he redeem'd from prison. All these

  Owe their estates unto him.

Serv.   My lord,

  They have all been touch'd, and found base metal, for

  They all have denied him.

Sem.   How ? have they denied him ?

  Has Ventidius and Lucullus denied him,

  And does he send to me ? Three ? hum !

  It shows but little love, or judgement in him.   10

  Must I be his last refuge ? His friends, like phy-
   sicians,

  Thrive, give him over: must I take the cure upon me ? †

  Has much disgrac'd me in 't, I'm angry at him,

  That might have known my place. I see no sense
   for 't,

  But his occasions might have woo'd me first ;

46

For, in my conscience, I was the first man
That e'er received gift from him,
And does he think so backwardly of me now,
That I'll requite it last?   No:
So it may prove an argument of laughter   20
To the rest, and 'mongst lords I be thought a fool.
I'd rather than the worth of thrice the sum,
Had sent to me first, but for my mind's sake;
I'd such a courage to do him good.   But now
    return,
And with their faint reply this answer join;
Who bates mine honour shall not know my coin.

                            Exit

Serv. Excellent!   Your lordship's a goodly villain: the
devil knew not what he did when he made man
politic; he crossed himself by't: and I cannot
think but in the end the villanies of man will set   30
him clear.   How fairly this lord strives to appear
foul! takes virtuous copies to be wicked: like those
that under hot ardent zeal would set whole realms
on fire,
Of such a nature is his politic love.
This was my lord's best hope; now all are fled,
Save only the gods.   Now his friends are dead,
Doors, that were ne'er acquainted with their wards

Many a bounteous year, must be employ'd
Now to guard sure their master: 4(
And this is all a liberal course allows,
Who cannot keep his wealth must keep his house.

Exit

SCENE IV

A hall in Timon's house

*Enter two Servants of Varro, and the Servant of Lucius,
meeting Titus, Hortensius, and other Servants of Timon's
creditors, waiting his coming out*

First Var. Serv. Well met; good morrow, Titus and
    Hortensius.

Tit. The like to you, kind Varro.

Hor.   Lucius!
What, do we meet together?

Luc. Serv.   Ay, and I think
One business does command us all. For mine
Is money.

Tit. So is theirs, and ours.

Enter Philotus

Luc. Serv.   And, sir, Philotus too!

Phi. Good day at once.

48

uc. Serv.   Welcome, good brother.
    What do you think the hour?

_hi._   Labouring for nine.

uc. Serv. So much?

_hi._   Is not my lord seen yet?

uc. Serv.   Not yet.

_hi._ I wonder on't, he was wont to shine at seven.   10

uc. Serv. Ay, but the days are wax'd shorter with him:
    You must consider that a prodigal course
    Is like the sun's, but not like his recoverable,
    I fear
    'Tis deepest winter in Lord Timon's purse,
    That is, one may reach deep enough, and yet
    Find little.

_hi._   I am of your fear for that.

_it._ I'll show you how to observe a strange event:
    Your lord sends now for money?

lor.   Most true, he does.

_it._ And he wears jewels now of Timon's gift,   20
    For which I wait for money.

lor. It is against my heart.

uc. Serv.   Mark, how strange it shows,
    Timon, in this, should pay more than he owes:
    And e'en as if your lord should wear rich jewels,
    And send for money for 'em.

Hor. I'm weary of this charge, the gods can witness:
    I know my lord hath spent of Timon's wealth,
    And now ingratitude makes it worse than stealth.

First Var. Serv. Yes, mine's three thousand crowns:
    what's yours?

Luc. Serv. Five thousand mine.   30

First Var. Serv. 'Tis much deep, and it should seem by
    the sum
    Your master's confidence was above mine,
    Else surely his had equall'd.

Enter Flaminius

Tit. One of Lord Timon's men.

Luc. Serv. Flaminius! Sir, a word: pray, is my lord
    ready to come forth?

Flam. No, indeed he is not.

Tit. We attend his lordship: pray, signify so much.

Flam. I need not tell him that, he knows you are too
    diligent.   *Exit* 40

Enter Flavius in a cloak, muffled

Luc. Serv. Ha! is not that his steward muffled so?
    He goes away in a cloud: call him, call him.

Tit. Do you hear, sir?

Sec. Var. Serv. By your leave, sir,—

Fla. What do ye ask of me, my friend?

Tit. We wait for certain money here, sir.

50

Fla.   Ay,

    If money were as certain as your waiting,

    'Twere sure enough.

    Why then preferr'd you not your sums and bills,

    When your false masters ate of my lord's meat?   **50**

    Then they could smile, and fawn upon his debts,

    And take down the interest into their gluttonous maws.

    You do yourselves but wrong, to stir me up,

    Let me pass quietly :

    Believe 't, my lord and I have made an end,

    I have no more to reckon, he to spend.

Luc. Serv. Ay, but this answer will not serve.

Fla. If 'twill not serve, 'tis not so base as you,

    For you serve knaves.   *Exit*

First Var. Serv. How? what does his cashier'd worship **60**

    mutter?

Sec. Var. Serv. No matter what, he's poor, and that's

    revenge enough. Who can speak broader than

    he that has no house to put his head in? Such

    may rail against great buildings.

Enter Servilius

Tit. O, here's Servilius: now we shall know some

    answer.

Ser. If I might beseech you, gentlemen, to repair some

    other hour, I should derive much from 't. For,

take 't of my soul, my lord leans wondrously to   7
discontent: his comfortable temper has forsook
him, he 's much out of health, and keeps his
chamber.

Luc. Serv. Many do keep their chambers are not sick:
And if it be so far beyond his health,
Methinks he should the sooner pay his debts,
And make a clear way to the gods.

Ser.   Good gods !

Tit. We cannot take this for answer, sir.

Flam. (*within*) Servilius, help ! My lord ! my lord !

    Enter Timon, in a rage ; Flaminius following

Tim. What, are my doors oppos'd against my passage ?   80
Have I been ever free, and must my house
Be my retentive enemy ? my gaol ?
The place which I have feasted, does it now,
(Like all mankind) show me an iron heart ?

Luc. Serv. Put in now, Titus.

Tit. My lord, here is my bill.

Luc. Serv. Here 's mine.

Hor. And mine, my lord.

Both Var. Serv. And ours, my lord.

Phi. All our bills.   90

Tim. Knock me down with 'em, cleave me to the girdle.

Luc. Serv. Alas, my lord,—

Tim. Cut my heart in sums.

Tit. Mine, fifty talents.

Tim. Tell out my blood.

Luc. Serv. Five thousand crowns, my lord.

Tim. Five thousand drops pays that. What yours?—
and yours?

First Var. Serv. My lord,—

Sec. Var. Serv. My lord,—   100

Tim. Tear me, take me, and the gods fall upon you! *Exit*

Hor. Faith, I perceive our masters may throw their caps
at their money, these debts may well be called
desperate ones, for a madman owes 'em.   *Exeunt*

Re-enter Timon and Flavius

Tim. They have e'en put my breath from me, the slaves.
Creditors? devils!

Fla. My dear lord,—

Tim. What if it should be so?

Fla. My lord,—

Tim. I'll have it so. My steward!   110

Fla. Here, my lord.

Tim. So fitly? Go, bid all my friends again,
Lucius, Lucullus, and Sempronius: all: †
I'll once more feast the rascals.

Fla.   O my lord,
You only speak from your distracted soul;

There's not so much left, to furnish out
A moderate table.

Tim.   Be it not in thy care; go,
I charge thee, invite them all, let in the tide
Of knaves once more; my cook and I'll provide.

                                        Exeunt

SCENE V

The Senate-house

Enter three Senators

First Sen. My lord, you have my voice; to't: the fault's
Bloody; 'tis necessary he should die:
Nothing emboldens sin so much as mercy.

Sec. Sen. Most true; the law shall bruise 'em.

                    Enter Alcibiades, attended

Alc. Honour, health, and compassion to the senate!

First Sen. Now, captain?

Alc. I am an humble suitor to your virtues;
For pity is the virtue of the law,
And none but tyrants use it cruelly.
It pleases time and fortune to lie heavy
Upon a friend of mine, who in hot blood   10

Hath stepp'd into the law ; which is past depth
To those that (without heed) do plunge into 't.
He is a man, (setting his fate aside)
Of comely virtues,
Nor did he soil the fact with cowardice
(An honour in him which buys out his fault)
But with a noble fury, and fair spirit,
Seeing his reputation touch'd to death,
He did oppose his foe :   20
And with such sober and unnoted passion
He did behoove his anger, ere 'twas spent,   †
As if he had but prov'd an argument.

First Sen. You undergo too strict a paradox,
Striving to make an ugly deed look fair :
Your words have took such pains, as if they labour'd
To bring manslaughter into form, and set quarrelling
Upon the head of valour ; which indeed
Is valour misbegot, and came into the world
When sects and factions were newly born.   30
He 's truly valiant, that can wisely suffer
The worst that man can breathe, and make his wrongs
His outsides, to wear them like his raiment, carelessly
And ne'er prefer his injuries to his heart,
To bring it into danger.
If wrongs be evils and enforce us kill,

     What folly 'tis to hazard life for ill !

Alc. My lord,—

First Sen.   You cannot make gross sins look clear :
     To revenge is no valour, but to bear.

Alc. My lords, then, under favour, pardon me,   40
     If I speak like a captain.
     Why do fond men expose themselves to battle,
     And not endure all threats ? sleep upon 't,
     And let the foes quietly cut their throats,
     Without repugnancy ?   If there be
     Such valour in the bearing, what make we
     Abroad ?   Why then, women are more valiant
     That stay at home, if bearing carry it :
     And the ass more captain than the lion ? the fellow
     Loaden with irons wiser than the judge ?   50
     If wisdom be in suffering.   O my lords,
     As you are great, be pitifully good :
     Who cannot condemn rashness in cold blood ?
     To kill, I grant, is sin's extremest gust,
     But in defence, by mercy, 'tis most just.
     To be in anger is impiety ;
     But who is man that is not angry ?
     Weigh but the crime with this.

Sec. Sen. You breathe in vain.

Alc.   In vain ?   His service done

At Lacedæmon, and Byzantium,   60
Were a sufficient briber for his life.

First Sen. What's that?

Alc.   I say, my lords, has done fair service,
And slain in fight many of your enemies:
How full of valour did he bear himself
In the last conflict, and made plenteous wounds!

Sec. Sen. He has made too much plenty with 'em;
He's a sworn rioter, he has a sin
That often drowns him, and takes his valour prisoner.
If there were no foes, that were enough
To overcome him.   In that beastly fury   70
He has been known to commit outrages,
And cherish factions.   'Tis inferr'd to us,
His days are foul, and his drink dangerous.

First Sen. He dies.

Alc.   Hard fate! he might have died in war.
My lords, if not for any parts in him,
Though his right arm might purchase his own time,
And be in debt to none, yet, more to move you,
Take my deserts to his, and join 'em both:
And, for I know your reverend ages love
Security, I'll pawn my victories, all   80
My honour to you, upon his good returns.
If by this crime he owes the law his life,

Why, let the war receive 't in valiant gore,
For law is strict, and war is nothing more.

First Sen. We are for law, he dies, urge it no more,
On height of our displeasure : friend, or brother,
He forfeits his own blood that spills another.

Alc. Must it be so ? it must not be : my lords,
I do beseech you, know me.

Sec. Sen. How ?   90

Alc. Call me to your remembrances.

Third Sen. What ?

Alc. I cannot think but your age has forgot me,
It could not else be I should prove so base,
To sue and be denied such common grace :
My wounds ache at you.

First Sen.   Do you dare our anger ?
'Tis in few words, but spacious in effect :
We banish thee for ever.

Alc.   Banish me ?
Banish your dotage, banish usury,
That makes the senate ugly.   100

First Sen. If, after two days' shine, Athens contain thee,
Attend our weightier judgement.   And, not to swell
       our spirit,
He shall be executed presently.   *Exeunt Senators*

Alc. Now the gods keep you old enough, that you may live

58

Only in bone, that none may look on you !
I 'm worse than mad : I have kept back their foes,
While they have told their money, and let out
Their coin upon large interest ; I myself
Rich only in large hurts.   All those, for this ?
Is this the balsam, that the usuring senate   110
Pours into captains' wounds ?   Banishment !
It comes not ill : I hate not to be banish'd,
It is a cause worthy my spleen and fury,
That I may strike at Athens.   I 'll cheer up
My discontented troops, and lay for hearts ;
'Tis honour with most lands to be at odds,
Soldiers should brook as little wrongs as gods.   *Exit*

SCENE VI

A banqueting-room in Timon's house

Music.   Tables set out : Servants attending.   Enter divers
Lords, Senators and others, at several doors

First Lord. The good time of day to you, sir.
Sec. Lord. I also wish it to you : I think this honourable
lord did but try us this other day.
First Lord. Upon that were my thoughts tiring when we

encounter'd : I hope it is not so low with him as
he made it seem in the trial of his several friends.

Sec. Lord. It should not be, by the persuasion of his new
feasting.

First Lord. I should think so. He hath sent me an
earnest inviting, which many my near occasions   10
did urge me to put off : but he hath conjur'd me
beyond them, and I must needs appear.

Sec. Lord. In like manner was I in debt to my importunate
business, but he would not hear my excuse. I am
sorry, when he sent to borrow of me, that my
provision was out.

First Lord. I am sick of that grief too, as I understand
how all things go.

Sec. Lord. Every man here's so : what would he have
borrowed of you ?   20

First Lord. A thousand pieces.

Sec. Lord. A thousand pieces ?

First Lord. What of you ?

Sec. Lord. He sent to me, sir,—Here he comes.

Enter Timon and Attendants

Tim. With all my heart, gentlemen both ; and how fare
you ?

First Lord. Ever at the best, hearing well of your lordship.

Sec. Lord. The swallow follows not summer more willing
 than we your lordship.   30

Tim. (aside) Nor more willingly leaves winter, such
 summer-birds are men.—Gentlemen, our dinner
 will not recompense this long stay: feast your
 ears with the music awhile, if they will fare so
 harshly o' the trumpet's sound; we shall to 't
 presently.

First Lord. I hope it remains not unkindly with your
 lordship, that I return'd you an empty messenger.

Tim. O, sir, let it not trouble you.

Sec. Lord. My noble lord,—   40

Tim. Ay, my good friend, what cheer?

Sec. Lord. My most honourable lord, I am e'en sick of
 shame, that, when your lordship this other day sent
 to me, I was so unfortunate a beggar.

Tim. Think not on 't, sir.

Sec. Lord. If you had sent but two hours before—

Tim. Let it not cumber your better remembrance. (*The
 banquet brought in.*) Come, bring in all together.

Sec. Lord. All cover'd dishes!

First Lord. Royal cheer, I warrant you.   50

Third Lord. Doubt not that, if money and the season can
 yield it.

First Lord. How do you? What 's the news?

Third Lord. Alcibiades is banish'd : heard you of it ?

First and Sec. Lords. Alcibiades banish'd ?

Third Lord. 'Tis so, be sure of it.

First Lord. How ? how ?

Sec. Lord. I pray you, upon what ?

Tim. My worthy friends, will you draw near ?

Third Lord. I'll tell you more anon. Here's a noble   60
feast toward.

Sec. Lord. This is the old man still.

Third Lord. Will 't hold ? will 't hold ?

Sec. Lord. It does : but time will—and so—

Third Lord. I do conceive.

Tim. Each man to his stool, with that spur as he would
to the lip of his mistress : your diet shall be in all
places alike. Make not a city feast of it, to let
the meat cool, ere we can agree upon the first place.
Sit, sit. The gods require our thanks.   70

You great benefactors, sprinkle our society with
thankfulness. For your own gifts, make yourselves prais'd : but reserve still to give, lest your
deities be despis'd. Lend to each man enough,
that one need not lend to another. For, were your
godheads to borrow of men, men would forsake
the gods. Make the meat be belov'd, more than
the man that gives it. Let no assembly of twenty

be without a score of villains. If there sit twelve
women at the table, let a dozen of them be as they   80
are. The rest of your fees, O gods,—the senators
of Athens, together with the common lag of people,
—what is amiss in them, you gods, make suitable
for destruction. For these my present friends, as
they are to me nothing, so in nothing bless them,
and to nothing are they welcome.

Uncover, dogs, and lap.

Some speak. What does his lordship mean?

Some other. I know not.

> *The dishes are uncovered and seen to be*
> *full of warm water*

Tim. May you a better feast never behold,   90
　　　You knot of mouth-friends! smoke and luke-warm
　　　　　water
　　　Is your perfection. This is Timon's last
　　　Who stuck and spangled you with flatteries,
　　　Washes it off, and sprinkles in your faces
　　　Your reeking villainy. *(Throwing the water in their faces)*
　　　　　　　　Live loath'd, and long,
　　　Most smiling, smooth, detested parasites,
　　　Courteous destroyers, affable wolves, meek bears:
　　　You fools of fortune, trencher-friends, time's flies,
　　　Cap-and-knee slaves, vapours, and minute-jacks!

63

Of man and beast the infinite malady   10c
Crust you quite o'er!   What, dost thou go?
Soft, take thy physic first; thou too, and thou:
Stay, I will lend thee money, borrow none.
What? all in motion?   Henceforth be no feast,
Whereat a villain's not a welcome guest.
Burn, house! sink, Athens! henceforth hated be
Of Timon man and all humanity!   *Exit*

Re-enter the Lords, Senators, &c.

First Lord. How now, my lords!

Sec. Lord. Know you the quality of Lord Timon's fury?

Third Lord. Push! did you see my cap?   11c

Fourth Lord. I have lost my gown.

First Lord. He's but a mad lord, and nought but humours
    sways him.   He gave me a jewel th' other day, and
    now he has beat it out of my hat.   Did you see my
    jewel?

Third Lord. Did you see my cap?

Sec. Lord. Here 'tis.

Fourth Lord. Here lies my gown.

First Lord. Let's make no stay.

Sec. Lord. Lord Timon's mad.

Third Lord.   I feel 't upon my bones.   120

Fourth Lord. One day he gives us diamonds, next day
        stones.   *Exeunt*

Act Fourth

SCENE I

Without the walls of Athens

Enter Timon

Tim. Let me look back upon thee. O thou wall,
 That girdles in those wolves, dive in the earth,
 And fence not Athens ! Matrons, turn incontinent,
 Obedience fail in children : slaves and fools
 Pluck the grave wrinkled senate from the bench,
 And minister in their steads ; to general filths
 Convert o' the instant green virginity,
 Do 't in your parents' eyes ! Bankrupts, hold fast,
 Rather than render back ; out with your knives,
 And cut your trusters' throats ! Bound servants, steal ! 10
 Large-handed robbers your grave masters are,
 And pill by law. Maid, to thy master's bed,
 Thy mistress is o' the brothel. Son of sixteen,
 Pluck the lin'd crutch from thy old limping sire,
 With it beat out his brains ! Piety, and fear,
 Religion to the gods, peace, justice, truth,
 Domestic awe, night-rest, and neighbourhood,

Instruction, manners, mysteries, and trades,
Degrees, observances, customs, and laws,
Decline to your confounding contraries.   2
And yet confusion live : plagues incident to men,
Your potent and infectious fevers, heap
On Athens, ripe for stroke ! Thou cold sciatica,
Cripple our senators, that their limbs may halt
As lamely as their manners ! Lust, and liberty
Creep in the minds and marrows of our youth,
That 'gainst the stream of virtue they may strive,
And drown themselves in riot ! Itches, blains,
Sow all the Athenian bosoms, and their crop
Be general leprosy : breath, infect breath,   3
That their society (as their friendship) may
Be merely poison ! Nothing I 'll bear from thee
But nakedness, thou detestable town,
Take thou that too, with multiplying bans !
Timon will to the woods, where he shall find
The unkindest beast more kinder than mankind.
The gods confound—hear me, you good gods all !—
The Athenians both within and out that wall !
And grant, as Timon grows, his hate may grow
To the whole race of mankind, high and low !   4
Amen.   *Exit*

SCENE II

Athens. Timon's house

Enter Flavius, with two or three Servants

First Serv. Hear you, master steward, where's our master?
    Are we undone? cast off? nothing remaining?

Fla. Alack, my fellows, what should I say to you?
    Let me be recorded by the righteous gods,
    I am as poor as you.

First Serv.   Such a house broke?
    So noble a master fall'n, all gone, and not
    One friend to take his fortune by the arm,
    And go along with him?

Sec. Serv.   As we do turn our backs
    From our companion, thrown into his grave,
    So his familiars to his buried fortunes   **10**
    Slink all away, leave their false vows with him
    Like empty purses pick'd; and his poor self,
    A dedicated beggar to the air,
    With his disease of all-shunn'd poverty,
    Walks, like contempt, alone. More of our fellows.

Enter other Servants

Fla. All broken implements of a ruin'd house.

Third Serv. Yet do our hearts wear Timon's livery,

That see I by our faces: we are fellows still,
Serving alike in sorrow: leak'd is our bark,
And we, poor mates, stand on the dying deck,   20
Hearing the surges threat: we must all part
Into this sea of air.

Fla.   Good fellows all,
The latest of my wealth I'll share amongst you.
Wherever we shall meet, for Timon's sake
Let's yet be fellows.   Let's shake our heads, and say,
As 'twere a knell unto our master's fortunes,
'We have seen better days.'   Let each take some:
Nay, put out all your hands: not one word more,
Thus part we rich in sorrow, parting poor.

Servants embrace, and part several ways

O, the fierce wretchedness that glory brings us!   30
Who would not wish to be from wealth exempt,
Since riches point to misery and contempt?
Who would be so mock'd with glory? or to live
But in a dream of friendship,
To have his pomp, and all what state compounds,
But only painted like his varnish'd friends?
Poor honest lord, brought low by his own heart,
Undone by goodness!   Strange, unusual blood,
When man's worst sin is, he does too much good!
Who then dares to be half so kind again?   40

For bounty, that makes gods, does still mar men.
My dearest lord, blest to be most accurs'd,
Rich only to be wretched ; thy great fortunes
Are made thy chief afflictions.   Alas (kind lord)
He 's flung in rage from this ingrateful seat
Of monstrous friends : nor has he with him to
Supply his life, or that which can command it :
I 'll follow and inquire him out.
I 'll ever serve his mind, with my best will ;
Whilst I have gold, I 'll be his steward still.   *Exit* 50

SCENE III

and

Act Fifth : SCENE I

The woods

Enter Timon

Tim. O blessed breeding sun, draw from the earth
  Rotten humidity : below thy sister's orb
  Infect the air !   Twinn'd brothers of one womb,
  Whose procreation, residence, and birth
  Scarce is dividant, touch them with several fortunes

The greater scorns the lesser. Not nature,
(To whom all sores lay siege) can bear great fortune
But by contempt of nature.
Raise me this beggar, and deny 't that lord,
The senator shall bear contempt hereditary,   10
The beggar native honour.
It is the pasture lards the rother's sides,
The want that makes him lean. Who dares, who
        dares,
In purity of manhood stand upright,
And say ' This man's a flatterer' ? if one be,
So are they all : for every grise of fortune
Is smooth'd by that below. The learned pate
Ducks to the golden fool. All's obliquy ;
There's nothing level in our cursed natures
But direct villainy. Therefore be abhorr'd,   20
All feasts, societies, and throngs of men !
His semblable, yea, himself, Timon disdains :
Destruction fang mankind ! Earth yield me roots,
                                          Digging
Who seeks for better of thee, sauce his palate
With thy most operant poison ! What is here ?
Gold ? Yellow, glittering, precious gold ? No, gods,
I am no idle votarist : roots, you clear heavens !
Thus much of this will make black, white ; foul, fair ;

Wrong, right ; base, noble ; old, young ; coward,
    valiant.
Ha, you gods ! why this ? what this, you gods ?
    Why, this   30
Will lug your priests and servants from your sides ;
Pluck stout men's pillows from below their heads :
This yellow slave
Will knit and break religions, bless the accurs'd,
Make the hoar leprosy ador'd, place thieves,
And give them title, knee, and approbation
With senators on the bench : this is it
That makes the wapper'd widow wed again ;
She, whom the spital-house, and ulcerous sores
Would cast the gorge at, this embalms and spices 40
To the April day again.   Come, damn'd earth,
Thou common whore of mankind, that puts odds
Among the rout of nations, I will make thee
Do thy right nature.   (*March afar off.*)   Ha ? a drum ?
    Thou 'rt quick,
But yet I 'll bury thee : thou 'lt go (strong thief)
When gouty keepers of thee cannot stand :
Nay, stay thou out for earnest.   *Keeping some gold*
Enter Alcibiades, with drum and fife, in warlike manner ;
              Phrynia and Timandra

Alc.   What art thou there ? speak.

Tim. A beast as thou art. The canker gnaw thy heart,
For showing me again the eyes of man !

Alc. What is thy name ? Is man so hateful to thee,   5
That art thyself a man ?

Tim. I am misanthropos, and hate mankind.
For thy part, I do wish thou wert a dog,
That I might love thee something.

Alc.   I know thee well :
But in thy fortunes am unlearn'd and strange.

Tim. I know thee too, and more than that I know thee
I not desire to know. Follow thy drum !
With man's blood paint the ground gules, gules :
Religious canons, civil laws are cruel,
Then what should war be ? This fell whore of thine 6
Hath in her more destruction than thy sword,
For all her cherubin look.

Phr.   Thy lips rot off !

Tim. I will not kiss thee, then the rot returns
To thine own lips again.

Alc. How came the noble Timon to this change ?

Tim. As the moon does, by wanting light to give :
But then renew I could not like the moon,
There were no suns to borrow of.

Alc.   Noble Timon,
What friendship may I do thee ?

Tim.   None, but to
    Maintain my opinion.   70

Alc. What is it, Timon ?

Tim. Promise me friendship, but perform none. If thou
    wilt not promise, the gods plague thee, for thou art
    a man : if thou dost perform, confound thee, for
    thou art a man !

Alc. I have heard in some sort of thy miseries.

Tim. Thou saw'st them when I had prosperity.

Alc. I see them now ; then was a blessed time.

Tim. As thine is now, held with a brace of harlots.

Timan. Is this the Athenian minion, whom the world   80
    Voic'd so regardfully ?

Tim.   Art thou Timandra ?

Timan. Yes.

Tim. Be a whore still : they love thee not that use thee ;
    Give them diseases, leaving with thee their lust.
    Make use of thy salt hours, season the slaves
    For tubs and baths, bring down rose-cheeked youth
    To the tub-fast, and the diet.

Timan.   Hang thee, monster !

Alc. Pardon him, sweet Timandra, for his wits
    Are drown'd and lost in his calamities.
    I have but little gold of late, brave Timon,   90
    The want whereof doth daily make revolt

In my penurious band : I have heard, and griev'd,
How cursed Athens, mindless of thy worth,
Forgetting thy great deeds, when neighbour states,
But for thy sword and fortune, trod upon them—
Tim. I prithee, beat thy drum, and get thee gone.
Alc. I am thy friend, and pity thee, dear Timon.
Tim. How dost thou pity him whom thou dost trouble ?
I had rather be alone.
Alc.   Why, fare thee well :
Here is some gold for thee.
Tim.   Keep it, I cannot eat it.   10
Alc. When I have laid proud Athens on a heap—
Tim. Warr'st thou 'gainst Athens ?
Alc.   Ay, Timon, and have cause.
Tim. The gods confound them all in thy conquest,
And thee after, when thou hast conquered !
Alc. Why me, Timon ?
Tim.   That by killing of villains
Thou wast born to conquer my country.
Put up thy gold. Go on, here's gold, go on ;
Be as a planetary plague, when Jove
Will o'er some high-vic'd city hang his poison
In the sick air : let not thy sword skip one :   110
Pity not honour'd age for his white beard,
He is an usurer. Strike me the counterfeit matron,

It is her habit only, that is honest,
Herself's a bawd. Let not the virgin's cheek
Make soft thy trenchant sword ; for those milk-paps,
That through the window-bars bore at men's eyes,
Are not within the leaf of pity writ,
But set them down horrible traitors. Spare not the babe
Whose dimpled smiles from fools exhaust their mercy ;
Think it a bastard, whom the oracle   120
Hath doubtfully pronounc'd the throat shall cut,
And mince it sans remorse. Swear against objects,
Put armour on thine ears ; and on thine eyes,
Whose proof nor yells of mothers, maids, nor babes,
Nor sight of priests in holy vestments bleeding,
Shall pierce a jot. There's gold to pay thy soldiers,
Make large confusion : and, thy fury spent,
Confounded be thyself ! Speak not, be gone.

Alc. Hast thou gold yet ? I'll take the gold thou giv'st me,
Not all thy counsel.   130

Tim. Dost thou or dost thou not, heaven's curse upon thee !

Phr. and Timan. Give us some gold, good Timon : hast thou
more ?

Tim. Enough to make a whore forswear her trade,
And to make whores, a bawd. Hold up, you sluts,
Your aprons mountant ; you are not oathable,
Although I know you'll swear, terribly swear

Into strong shudders and to heavenly agues
The immortal gods that hear you.   Spare your oaths:
I 'll trust to your conditions, be whores still.
And he whose pious breath seeks to convert you,   14(
Be strong in whore, allure him, burn him up,
Let your close fire predominate his smoke,
And be no turncoats: yet may your pains, six months,
Be quite contrary: and thatch your poor thin roofs
With burdens of the dead, (some that were hang'd)
No matter:—wear them, betray with them; whore still,
Paint till a horse may mire upon your face:
A pox of wrinkles!

Phr. and Timan. Well, more gold, what then?
Believe 't that we 'll do any thing for gold.   15(

Tim. Consumptions sow
In hollow bones of man, strike their sharp shins,
And mar men's spurring.   Crack the lawyer's voice,
That he may never more false title plead,
Nor sound his quillets shrilly: hoar the flamen,
That scolds against the quality of flesh,
And not believes himself.   Down with the nose,
Down with it flat, take the bridge quite away
Of him that, his particular to foresee,
Smells from the general weal.   Make curl'd-pate
        ruffians bald,   16(

And let the unscarr'd braggarts of the war
Derive some pain from you.   Plague all,
That your activity may defeat and quell
The source of all erection.   There's more gold.
Do you damn others, and let this damn you,
And ditches grave you all!

Phr. and Timan. More counsel with more money, boun-
      teous Timon.

Tim. More whore, more mischief first; I have given you
      earnest.

Alc. Strike up the drum towards Athens; farewell, Timon:
If I thrive well, I'll visit thee again.   170

Tim. If I hope well, I'll never see thee more.

Alc. I never did thee harm.

Tim. Yes, thou spok'st well of me.

Alc.   Call'st thou that harm?

Tim. Men daily find it.   Get thee away, and take
Thy beagles with thee.

Alc.   We but offend him; strike!

              Drums beat.   Exeunt Alcibiades,
                    Phrynia, and Timandra

Tim. That nature, being sick of man's unkindness,
Should yet be hungry!   Common mother, thou
                        Digging

Whose womb unmeasurable, and infinite breast

Teems and feeds all: whose self-same mettle,
Whereof thy proud child, arrogant man, is puff'd,   180
Engenders the black toad, and adder blue,
The gilded newt, and eyeless venom'd worm,
With all the abhorred births below crisp heaven,
Whereon Hyperion's quickening fire doth shine:
Yield him, who all the human sons do hate,   †
From forth thy plenteous bosom, one poor root:
Ensear thy fertile and conceptious womb,
Let it no more bring out ingrateful man!
Go great with tigers, dragons, wolves, and bears;
Teem with new monsters, whom thy upward face   190
Hath to the marbled mansion all above
Never presented!—O, a root! dear thanks!—
Dry up thy marrows, vines, and plough-torn leas,
Whereof ingrateful man with liquorish draughts
And morsels unctuous greases his pure mind,
That from it all consideration slips!

Enter Apemantus

More man? plague, plague!
Ape. I was directed hither.   Men report
      Thou dost affect my manners, and dost use them.
Tim. 'Tis then because thou dost not keep a dog,   200
      Whom I would imitate.   Consumption catch thee!
Ape. This is in thee a nature but infected,

A poor unmanly melancholy sprung
From change of fortune.   Why this spade? this place?
This slave-like habit, and these looks of care?
Thy flatterers yet wear silk, drink wine, lie soft,
Hug their diseas'd perfumes, and have forgot
That ever Timon was.   Shame not these woods
By putting on the cunning of a carper.
Be thou a flatterer now, and seek to thrive   210
By that which has undone thee; hinge thy knee,
And let his very breath whom thou 'lt observe
Blow off thy cap: praise his most vicious strain,
And call it excellent: thou wast told thus:
Thou gav'st thine ears (like tapsters that bade welcome)
To knaves, and all approachers: 'tis most just
That thou turn rascal, hadst thou wealth again,
Rascals should have 't.   Do not assume my likeness.

Tim. Were I like thee, I 'ld throw away myself.

Ape. Thou hast cast away thyself, being like thyself,   220
A madman so long, now a fool: what, think'st
That the bleak air, thy boisterous chamberlain,
Will put thy shirt on warm? will these moss'd trees,
That have outliv'd the eagle, page thy heels,
And skip when thou point'st out?   Will the cold brook,
Candied with ice, caudle thy morning taste
To cure thy o'er-night's surfeit?   Call the creatures,

Whose naked natures live in all the spite
Of wreakful heaven, whose bare unhoused trunks,
To the conflicting elements expos'd,   230
Answer mere nature : bid them flatter thee.
O, thou shalt find—

Tim.   A fool of thee : depart.

Ape. I love thee better now than ere I did.

Tim. I hate thee worse.

Ape.   Why ?

Tim.   Thou flatter'st misery.

Ape. I flatter not, but say thou art a caitiff.

Tim. Why dost thou seek me out ?

Ape.   To vex thee.

Tim. Always a villain's office, or a fool's.
Dost please thyself in 't ?

Ape.   Ay.

Tim.   What, a knave too ?

Ape. If thou didst put this sour cold habit on
To castigate thy pride, 'twere well : but thou   240
Dost it enforcedly : thou 'ldst courtier be again,
Wert thou not beggar : willing misery
Outlives incertain pomp, is crown'd before :
The one is filling still, never complete ;
The other, at high wish : best state, contentless,
Hath a distracted and most wretched being,

Worse than the worst, content.
Thou shouldst desire to die, being miserable.

Tim. Not by his breath that is more miserable.
Thou art a slave, whom Fortune's tender arm   250
With favour never clasp'd; but bred a dog.
Hadst thou like us from our first swath proceeded,
The sweet degrees that this brief world affords
To such as may the passive drugs of it
Freely command, thou wouldst have plung'd thyself
In general riot, melted down thy youth
In different beds of lust, and never learn'd
The icy precepts of respect, but follow'd
The sugar'd game before thee.   But myself,
Who had the world as my confectionary,   260
The mouths, the tongues, the eyes, and hearts of men,
At duty more than I could frame employment;
That numberless upon me stuck, as leaves
Do on the oak, have with one winter's brush
Fell from their boughs, and left me open, bare,
For every storm that blows.   I to bear this,
That never knew but better, is some burden:
Thy nature did commence in sufferance, time
Hath made thee hard in 't.   Why shouldst thou hate
      men?
They never flatter'd thee.   What hast thou given?   270

If thou wilt curse, thy father (that poor rag)
Must be thy subject, who in spite put stuff
To some she-beggar, and compounded thee
Poor rogue, hereditary.   Hence, be gone !
If thou hadst not been born the worst of men,
Thou hadst been a knave and flatterer.

Ape.   Art thou proud yet ?

Tim. Ay, that I am not thee.

Ape.   I, that I was
No prodigal.

Tim.   I, that I am one now.
Were all the wealth I have shut up in thee,
I 'ld give thee leave to hang it.   Get thee gone.   280
That the whole life of Athens were in this !
Thus would I eat it.   *Eating a root*

Ape.   Here, I will mend thy feast.
                                          Offering him a root

Tim. First mend my company, take away thyself.

Ape. So I shall mend mine own, by the lack of thine.

Tim. 'Tis not well mended so, it is but botch'd ;
If not, I would it were.

Ape. What wouldst thou have to Athens ?

Tim. Thee thither in a whirlwind : if thou wilt,
Tell them there I have gold, look, so I have.

Ape. Here is no use for gold.

Tim.   The best, and truest :   290

For here it sleeps, and does no hired harm.

Ape. Where liest o' nights, Timon ?

Tim.   Under that 's above me.

Where feed'st thou o' days, Apemantus ?

Ape. Where my stomach finds meat, or, rather where I
eat it.

Tim. Would poison were obedient, and knew my mind !

Ape. Where wouldst thou send it ?

Tim. To sauce thy dishes.

Ape. The middle of humanity thou never knewest, but
the extremity of both ends.   When thou wast in thy 300
gilt, and thy perfume, they mock'd thee for too much
curiosity ; in thy rags thou know'st none, but art
despis'd for the contrary.   There 's a medlar for
thee ; eat it.

Tim. On what I hate I feed not.

Ape. Dost hate a medlar ?

Tim. Ay, though it look like thee.

Ape. An thou hadst hated meddlers sooner, thou shouldst
have lov'd thyself better now.   What man didst
thou ever know unthrift that was belov'd after his 310
means ?

Tim. Who, without those means thou talk'st of, didst thou
ever know belov'd ?

*Ape.*Myself.

*Tim.*I understand thee : thou hadst some means to keep a dog.

*Ape.*What things in the world canst thou nearest compare to thy flatterers ?

*Tim.*Women nearest, but men—men are the things themselves. What wouldst thou do with the world, 320 Apemantus, if it lay in thy power ?

*Ape.*Give it the beasts, to be rid of the men.

*Tim.*Wouldst thou have thyself fall in the confusion of men, and remain a beast with the beasts ?

*Ape.*Ay, Timon.

*Tim.*A beastly ambition, which the gods grant thee t' attain to ! If thou wert the lion, the fox would beguile thee : if thou wert the lamb, the fox would eat thee : if thou wert the fox, the lion would suspect thee, when peradventure thou wert accus'd by the 330 ass : if thou wert the ass, thy dulness would torment thee ; and still thou livedst but as a breakfast to the wolf. If thou wert the wolf, thy greediness would afflict thee, and oft thou shouldst hazard thy life for thy dinner. Wert thou the unicorn, pride and wrath would confound thee, and make thine own self the conquest of thy fury. Wert thou a bear, thou wouldst be kill'd by the horse : wert thou a horse,

thou wouldst be seiz'd by the leopard : wert thou a
leopard, thou wert german to the lion, and the 340
spots of thy kindred were jurors on thy life.   All
thy safety were remotion, and thy defence absence.
What beast couldst thou be that were not subject
to a beast ? and what a beast art thou already, that
seest not thy loss in transformation !

*Ape.*If thou couldst please me with speaking to me,
thou mightst have hit upon it here : the common-
wealth of Athens is become a forest of beasts.

*Tim.*How has the ass broke the wall, that thou art out of
the city ? 350

*Ape.*Yonder comes a poet and a painter : the plague of
company light upon thee !   I will fear to catch it,
and give way.   When I know not what else to do,
I 'll see thee again.

*Tim.*When there is nothing living but thee, thou shalt
be welcome.   I had rather be a beggar's dog than
Apemantus.

*Ape.*Thou art the cap of all the fools alive.

*Tim.*Would thou wert clean enough to spit upon !

*Ape.*A plague on thee, thou art too bad to curse. 360

*Tim.*All villains that do stand by thee are pure.

*Ape.*There is no leprosy but what thou speak'st.

*Tim.*If I name thee,

I'll beat thee ; but I should infect my hands.

Ape. I would my tongue could rot them off !

Tim. Away, thou issue of a mangy dog,
  Choler does kill me, that thou art alive,
  I swoon to see thee.

Ape. Would thou wouldst burst !

Tim. Away, thou tedious rogue, I am sorry I shall lose 370
  a stone by thee.   *Throws a stone at him*

Ape. Beast !

Tim. Slave !

Ape. Toad !

Tim. Rogue, rogue, rogue !
  I am sick of this false world, and will love nought
  But even the mere necessities upon 't :
  Then, Timon, presently prepare thy grave :
  Lie where the light foam of the sea may beat
  Thy grave-stone daily, make thine epitaph,   380
  That death in me at others' lives may laugh.
  (*To the gold*) O thou sweet king-killer, and dear divorce
  'Twixt natural son and sire ; thou bright defiler
  Of Hymen's purest bed, thou valiant Mars,
  Thou ever young, fresh, lov'd, and delicate wooer,
  Whose blush doth thaw the consecrated snow
  That lies on Dian's lap ! thou visible god,
  That solder'st close impossibilities,

And mak'st them kiss; that speak'st with every tongue,
To every purpose: O thou touch of hearts,   390
Think thy slave man rebels, and by thy virtue
Set them into confounding odds, that beasts
May have the world in empire!

Ape.   Would 'twere so,
But not till I am dead.   I'll say thou hast gold:
Thou wilt be throng'd to shortly.

Tim.   Throng'd to?

Ape.   Ay.

Tim. Thy back, I prithee.

Ape.   Live, and love thy misery!

Tim. Long live so, and so die!   I am quit.

Ape. Moe things like men; eat, Timon, and abhor them.

                                                    Exit

Enter Banditti

First Ban. Where should he have this gold?   It is some
        poor fragment, some slender ort of his remainder: 400
        the mere want of gold, and the falling-from of his
        friends, drove him into this melancholy.

Sec. Ban. It is nois'd he hath a mass of treasure.

Third Ban. Let us make the assay upon him; if he care
        not for 't, he will supply us easily: if he covetously
        reserve it, how shall 's get it?

Sec. Ban. True, for he bears it not about him: 'tis hid.

First Ban. Is not this he?

Banditti. Where?

Sec. Ban. 'Tis his description. 410

Third Ban. He! I know him.

Banditti. Save thee, Timon.

Tim. Now, thieves?

Banditti. Soldiers, not thieves.

Tim. Both too, and women's sons.

Banditti. We are not thieves, but men that much do want.

Tim. Your greatest want is, you want much of meat:
 Why should you want? Behold, the earth hath roots:
 Within this mile break forth a hundred springs:
 The oaks bear mast, the briers scarlet heps, 420
 The bounteous housewife nature, on each bush,
 Lays her full mess before you. Want? why want?

First Ban. We cannot live on grass, on berries, water,
 As beasts, and birds, and fishes.

Tim. Nor on the beasts themselves, the birds, and fishes;
 You must eat men. Yet thanks I must you con,
 That you are thieves profess'd; that you work not
 In holier shapes: for there is boundless theft
 In limited professions. Rascal thieves,
 Here's gold. Go, suck the subtle blood o' the grape,
 Till the high fever seethe your blood to froth, 431
 And so 'scape hanging. Trust not the physician,

His antidotes are poison, and he slays
Moe than you rob : take wealth and lives together ;
Do villainy, do, since you protest to do 't,
Like workmen.   I 'll example you with thievery :
The sun 's a thief, and with his great attraction
Robs the vast sea.   The moon 's an arrant thief,
And her pale fire she snatches from the sun.
The sea 's a thief, whose liquid surge resolves   440
The moon into salt tears.   The earth 's a thief,
That feeds and breeds by a composture stol'n
From general excrement : each thing 's a thief.
The laws, your curb and whip, in their rough power
Has uncheck'd theft. Love not yourselves, away,
Rob one another, there 's more gold, cut throats,
All that you meet are thieves : to Athens go,
Break open shops, nothing can you steal,
But thieves do lose it : steal no less for this
I give you, and gold confound you howsoe'er :   450
Amen.

Third Ban. Has almost charm'd me from my profession,
by persuading me to it.

First Ban. 'Tis in the malice of mankind, that he thus
advises us, not to have us thrive in our mystery.

Sec. Ban. I 'll believe him as an enemy, and give over my
trade.

First Ban. Let us first see peace in Athens; there is no
    time so miserable but a man may be true.

                              Exeunt Banditti

                Enter Flavius

Fla. O you gods !   460
    Is yond despis'd and ruinous man my lord ?
    Full of decay and failing ?   O monument
    And wonder of good deeds, evilly bestow'd !
    What an alteration of honour
    Has desperate want made !
    What viler thing upon the earth than friends,
    Who can bring noblest minds to basest ends !
    How rarely does it meet with this time's guise,
    When man was wish'd to love his enemies !
    Grant I may ever love, and rather woo   470
    Those that would mischief me than those that do :
    Has caught me in his eye, I will present
    My honest grief unto him ; and, as my lord,
    Still serve him with my life.   My dearest master !
Tim. Away ! what art thou ?
Fla.   Have you forgot me, sir ?
Tim. Why dost ask that ? I have forgot all men.
    Then, if thou grant'st thou 'rt a man, I have forgot thee.
Fla. An honest poor servant of yours.

Tim. Then I know thee not :
I never had honest man about me ; ay, all   480
I kept were knaves, to serve-in meat to villains.

Fla. The gods are witness,
Ne'er did poor steward wear a truer grief
For his undone lord than mine eyes for you.

Tim. What, dost thou weep ? come nearer, then I love thee,
Because thou art a woman, and disclaim'st
Flinty mankind ; whose eyes do never give
But thorough lust and laughter.   Pity's sleeping :
Strange times, that weep with laughing, not with
            weeping !

Fla. I beg of you to know me, good my lord,   490
To accept my grief, and, whilst this poor wealth lasts,
To entertain me as your steward still.

Tim. Had I a steward
So true, so just, and now so comfortable ?
It almost turns my dangerous nature mild.
Let me behold thy face.   Surely, this man
Was born of woman.
Forgive my general and exceptless rashness,
You perpetual-sober gods ! I do proclaim
One honest man : mistake me not, but one :   500
No more, I pray, and he's a steward.
How fain would I have hated all mankind,

And thou redeem'st thyself.   But all save thee
I fell with curses.
Methinks thou art more honest now than wise:
For, by oppressing and betraying me,
Thou mightst have sooner got another service:
For many so arrive at second masters,
Upon their first lord's neck.   But tell me true
(For I must ever doubt, though ne'er so sure)   510
Is not thy kindness subtle, covetous,
If not a usuring kindness, and as rich men deal gifts,
Expecting in return twenty for one?

Fla. No, my most worthy master, in whose breast
Doubt and suspect, alas, are plac'd too late:
You should have fear'd false times, when you did feast:
Suspect still comes, where an estate is least.
That which I show, heaven knows, is merely love,
Duty, and zeal, to your unmatched mind,
Care of your food and living; and, believe it,   520
My most honour'd lord,
For any benefit that points to me,
Either in hope, or present, I 'ld exchange
For this one wish, that you had power and wealth
To requite me, by making rich yourself.

Tim. Look thee, 'tis so!   Thou singly honest man,
Here, take: the gods, out of my misery,

Have sent thee treasure.   Go, live rich and happy ;
But thus condition'd : thou shalt build from men :
Hate all, curse all, show charity to none,   530
But let the famish'd flesh slide from the bone
Ere thou relieve the beggar.   Give to dogs
What thou deniest to men.   Let prisons swallow 'em,
Debts wither 'em to nothing, be men like blasted
  woods,
And may diseases lick up their false bloods ;
And so farewell, and thrive.

Fla.   O, let me stay,
And comfort you, my master.

Tim.   If thou hat'st curses
Stay not : fly, whilst thou art blest and free :
Ne'er see thou man, and let me ne'er see thee.

           Exeunt severally

     Enter Poet and Painter

Pai. As I took note of the place, it cannot be far where
he abides.

Po. What's to be thought of him ?   does the rumour
hold for true, that he 's so full of gold ?

Pai. Certain :   Alcibiades   reports   it ;   Phrynia   and

       93

Timandra had gold of him. He likewise enrich'd
poor straggling soldiers, with great quantity. 'Tis
said he gave unto his steward a mighty sum.

Po. Then this breaking of his has been but a try for
his friends?

10

Pai. Nothing else: you shall see him a palm in Athens
again, and flourish with the highest: therefore 'tis
not amiss we tender our loves to him in this suppos'd
distress of his: it will show honestly in us, and is
very likely to load our purposes with what they
travail for, if it be a just and true report that goes
of his having.

Po. What have you now to present unto him?

Pai. Nothing at this time but my visitation: only I
will promise him an excellent piece.

20

Po. I must serve him so too; tell him of an intent that's
coming toward him.

Pai. Good as the best. Promising is the very air o' the
time; it opens the eyes of expectation: performance
is ever the duller for his act; and, but in the plainer
and simpler kind of people, the deed of saying is
quite out of use. To promise is most courtly and
fashionable; performance is a kind of will or
testament which argues a great sickness in his
judgement that makes it.

30

Enter Timon from his cave

Tim.(*aside*) Excellent workman, thou canst not paint a
      man so bad as is thyself.

Po. I am thinking what I shall say I have provided for
      him : it must be a personating of himself ; a satire
      against the softness of prosperity, with a discovery
      of the infinite flatteries that follow youth and
      opulency.

Tim.(*aside*) Must thou needs stand for a villain in thine
      own work ? wilt thou whip thine own faults in
      other men ? Do so, I have gold for thee.   40

Po. Nay, let 's seek him.
      Then do we sin against our own estate,
      When we may profit meet, and come too late.

Pai. True :
      When the day serves, before black-corner'd night,
      Find what thou want'st, by free and offer'd light.
      Come.

Tim.(*aside*) I 'll meet you at the turn. What a god 's gold,
      That he is worshipp'd in a baser temple
      Than where swine feed !   50
      'Tis thou that rigg'st the bark, and plough'st the foam,
      Settlest admired reverence in a slave ;
      To thee be worship ! and thy saints for aye
      Be crown'd with plagues, that thee alone obey !

Fit I meet them. *Coming forward*

Po. Hail, worthy Timon!

Pai. Our late noble master!

Tim. Have I once liv'd to see two honest men?

Po. Sir,

Having often of your open bounty tasted,
Hearing you were retir'd, your friends fall'n off, 60
Whose thankless natures (O abhorred spirits!)
Not all the whips of heaven are large enough—
What! to you,
Whose star-like nobleness gave life and influence
To their whole being? I am rapt, and cannot cover
The monstrous bulk of this ingratitude
With any size of words.

Tim. Let it go naked, men may see 't the better:
You that are honest, by being what you are,
Make them best seen, and known.

Pai. He and myself 70
Have travail'd in the great shower of your gifts,
And sweetly felt it.

Tim. Ay, you are honest men.

Pai. We are hither come to offer you our service.

Tim. Most honest men: why, how shall I requite you?
Can you eat roots, and drink cold water? no.

Both. What we can do, we 'll do to do you service.

Tim. Ye 're honest men, ye 've heard that I have gold,
      I am sure you have, speak truth, ye 're honest men.

Pai. So it is said, my noble lord, but therefore
      Came not my friend nor I.   80

Tim. Good honest men !   Thou draw'st a counterfeit
      Best in all Athens, thou 'rt indeed the best,
      Thou counterfeit'st most lively.

Pai.   So, so, my lord.

Tim. E'en so, sir, as I say.   And, for thy fiction,
      Why, thy verse swells with stuff so fine and smooth
      That thou art even natural in thine art.
      But, for all this, my honest-natur'd friends,
      I must needs say you have a little fault,
      Marry, 'tis not monstrous in you, neither wish I
      You take much pains to mend.

Both.   Beseech your honour   90
      To make it known to us.

Tim.   You 'll take it ill.

Both. Most thankfully, my lord.

Tim.   Will you, indeed ?

Both. Doubt it not, worthy lord.

Tim. There 's never a one of you but trusts a knave,
      That mightily deceives you.

Both.   Do we, my lord ?

Tim. Ay, and you hear him cog, see him dissemble,

Know his gross patchery, love him, feed him,
Keep in your bosom, yet remain assur'd
That he's a made-up villain.

Pai. I know none such, my lord.

Po.   Nor I.   100

Tim. Look you, I love you well, I'll give you gold,
Rid me these villains from your companies;
Hang them, or stab them, drown them in a draught,
Confound them by some course, and come to me,
I'll give you gold enough.

Both. Name them, my lord, let's know them.

Tim. You that way, and you this: but two in company:
Each man apart, all single, and alone,
Yet an arch-villain keeps him company
If, where thou art, two villains shall not be,   110
Come not near him. If thou wouldst not reside
But where one villain is, then him abandon.
Hence, pack, there's gold, you came for gold, ye slaves:
(*to Painter*) You have work for me; there's payment,
          hence!
(*to Poet*) You are an alchemist, make gold of that:
Out, rascal dogs!

                    Beats them out, and then retires into his cave
                    Enter Flavius and two Senators

Fla. It is vain that you would speak with Timon:

For he is set so only to himself,
That nothing but himself which looks like man
Is friendly with him.

First Sen.　　　　　Bring us to his cave.　　　　120
It is our part and promise to the Athenians
To speak with Timon.

Sec. Sen.　　　　　At all times alike
Men are not still the same : 'twas time and griefs
That fram'd him thus. Time, with his fairer hand,
Offering the fortunes of his former days,
The former man may make him : bring us to him,
And chance it as it may.

Fla.　　　　　Here is his cave :
Peace and content be here ! Lord Timon ! Timon !
Look out, and speak to friends : the Athenians
By two of their most reverend senate greet thee :　130
Speak to them, noble Timon.

　　　　Timon comes from his cave

*Tim.*Thou sun, that comforts, burn ! Speak, and be hang'd :
For each true word, a blister, and each false
Be as a cauterizing to the root o' the tongue,
Consuming it with speaking !

First Sen.　　　　　Worthy Timon,—

*Tim.*Of none but such as you, and you of Timon.

First Sen. The senators of Athens greet thee, Timon.

99

Tim. I thank them, and would send them back the plague,
Could I but catch it for them.

First Sen.   O, forget
What we are sorry for ourselves in thee.   140
The senators, with one consent of love,
Entreat thee back to Athens, who have thought
On special dignities, which vacant lie
For thy best use and wearing.

Sec. Sen.   They confess
Toward thee forgetfulness too general, gross ;
Which now the public body, which doth seldom
Play the recanter, feeling in itself
A lack of Timon's aid, hath sense withal
Of it own fall, restraining aid to Timon,   †
And send forth us, to make their sorrow'd render,   150
Together with a recompense more fruitful
Than their offence can weigh down by the dram,
Ay, even such heaps and sums of love and wealth,
As shall to thee blot out what wrongs were theirs,
And write in thee the figures of their love,
Ever to read them thine.

Tim.   You witch me in it :
Surprise me to the very brink of tears :
Lend me a fool's heart, and a woman's eyes,
And I 'll beweep these comforts, worthy senators.

First Sen. Therefore, so please thee to return with us,   160
    And of our Athens, thine and ours, to take
    The captainship, thou shalt be met with thanks,
    Allow'd with absolute power, and thy good name
    Live with authority : so soon we shall drive back
    Of Alcibiades the approaches wild,
    Who, like a boar too savage, doth root up
    His country's peace.

Sec. Sen.   And shakes his threatening sword
    Against the walls of Athens.

First Sen.   Therefore, Timon,—

Tim. Well, sir, I will ; therefore, I will, sir, thus :
    If Alcibiades kill my countrymen,   170
    Let Alcibiades know this of Timon,
    That Timon cares not.   But if he sack fair Athens,
    And take our goodly aged men by the beards,
    Giving our holy virgins to the stain
    Of contumelious, beastly, mad-brain'd war ;
    Then let him know, and tell him Timon speaks it,
    In pity of our aged, and our youth,
    I cannot choose but tell him that I care not,
    And let him take 't at worst : for their knives care not,
    While you have throats to answer.   For myself,   180
    There 's not a whittle in the unruly camp,
    But I do prize it at my love before

The reverend'st throat in Athens.   So I leave you
To the protection of the prosperous gods,
As thieves to keepers.

Fla.   Stay not, all's in vain

Tim. Why, I was writing of my epitaph,
It will be seen to-morrow.   My long sickness
Of health, and living, now begins to mend,
And nothing brings me all things.   Go, live still,
Be Alcibiades your plague, you his ;   190
And last so long enough !

First Sen.   We speak in vain.

Tim. But yet I love my country, and am not
One that rejoices in the common wreck,
As common bruit doth put it.

First Sen.   That 's well spoke.

Tim. Commend me to my loving countrymen,—

First Sen. These words become your lips as they pass
          thorough them.

Sec. Sen. And enter in our ears, like great triumphers
In their applauding gates.

Tim.   Commend me to them,
And tell them, that to ease them of their griefs,
Their fears of hostile strokes, their aches, losses,   200
Their pangs of love, with other incident throes
That nature's fragile vessel doth sustain

In life's uncertain voyage, I will some kindness do
    them,
I'll teach them to prevent wild Alcibiades' wrath.

First Sen. (*aside*) I like this well, he will return again.

Tim. I have a tree, which grows here in my close,
    That mine own use invites me to cut down,
    And shortly must I fell it.   Tell my friends,
    Tell Athens, in the sequence of degree,
    From high to low throughout, that whoso please   210
    To stop affliction, let him take his haste ;
    Come hither ere my tree hath felt the axe,
    And hang himself.   I pray you, do my greeting.

Fla. Trouble him no further, thus you still shall find him.

Tim. Come not to me again, but say to Athens,
    Timon hath made his everlasting mansion
    Upon the beached verge of the salt flood,
    Whom once a day with his embossed froth
    The turbulent surge shall cover ; thither come,
    And let my grave-stone be your oracle.   220
    Lips, let sour words go by, and language end :
    What is amiss, plague and infection mend !
    Graves only be men's works, and death their gain ;
    Sun, hide thy beams ; Timon hath done his reign.

                      Retires to his cave

First Sen. His discontents are unremoveably

  Coupled to nature.

Sec. Sen. Our hope in him is dead : let us return,
  And strain what other means is left unto us
  In our dear peril.

First Sen.   It requires swift foot.   *Exeunt*

SCENE II

Before the walls of Athens

Enter two Senators and a Messenger

First Sen. Thou hast painfully discover'd : are his files
  As full as thy report ?

Mes.   I have spoke the least.
  Besides, his expedition promises
  Present approach.

Sec. Sen. We stand much hazard, if they bring not Timon.

Mes. I met a courier, one mine ancient friend,
  Whom, though in general part we were oppos'd,
  Yet our old love made a particular force,
  And made us speak like friends. This man was riding
  From Alcibiades to Timon's cave,   10
  With letters of entreaty, which imported
  His fellowship i' the cause against your city,

In part for his sake mov'd.

First Sen.   Here come our brothers.

Enter Senators from Timon

Third Sen. No talk of Timon, nothing of him expect.
The enemies' drum is heard, and fearful scouring
Doth choke the air with dust : in, and prepare ;
Ours is the fall, I fear, our foes the snare.   *Exeunt*

SCENE III

The woods.   Timon's cave, and a rude tomb seen

Enter a Soldier, seeking Timon

Sol. By all description this should be the place.
Who's here? speak, ho !   No answer?   What is this?
Timon is dead, who hath outstretch'd his span :   †
Some beast read this ; there does not live a man.
Dead, sure, and this his grave ; what's on this tomb,
I cannot read ; the character I'll take with wax,
Our captain hath in every figure skill ;
An ag'd interpreter, though young in days :
Before proud Athens he's set down by this,
Whose fall the mark of his ambition is.   *Exit* 10

SCENE IV

Before the walls of Athens

Trumpets sound.   Enter Alcibiades with his powers

Alc. Sound to this coward and lascivious town
  Our terrible approach.   *A parley sounded*
    Enter Senators upon the walls
  Till now you have gone on and fill'd the time
  With all licentious measure, making your wills
  The scope of justice.   Till now, myself and such
  As slept within the shadow of your power
  Have wander'd with our travers'd arms, and breath'd
  Our sufferance vainly : now the time is flush,
  When crouching marrow in the bearer strong
  Cries, of itself, ' No more : ' now breathless wrong   10
  Shall sit and pant in your great chairs of ease,
  And pursy insolence shall break his wind
  With fear and horrid flight.
First Sen.   Noble, and young ;
  When thy first griefs were but a mere conceit,
  Ere thou hadst power, or we had cause of fear,
  We sent to thee, to give thy rages balm,
  To wipe out our ingratitude, with loves
  Above their quantity.

Sec. Sen.   So did we woo
          Transformed Timon to our city's love
          By humble message, and by promis'd means :   20
          We were not all unkind, nor all deserve
          The common stroke of war.

First Sen.   These walls of ours
          Were not erected by their hands from whom
          You have receiv'd your grief : nor are they such,
          That these great towers, trophies, and schools should fall
          For private faults in them.

Sec. Sen.   Nor are they living
          Who were the motives that you first went out ;
          Shame, that they wanted cunning, in excess
          Hath broke their hearts.   March, noble lord,
          Into our city with thy banners spread :   30
          By decimation and a tithed death,
          If thy revenges hunger for that food
          Which nature loathes, take thou the destin'd tenth,
          And by the hazard of the spotted die
          Let die the spotted.

First Sen.   All have not offended :
          For those that were, it is not square to take,
          On those that are, revenge : crimes, like lands
          Are not inherited ; then, dear countryman,
          Bring in thy ranks, but leave without thy rage,

Spare thy Athenian cradle, and those kin 40
Which in the bluster of thy wrath must fall
With those that have offended; like a shepherd,
Approach the fold, and cull the infected forth,
But kill not all together.

Sec. Sen.   What thou wilt,
Thou rather shalt enforce it with thy smile,
Than hew to 't with thy sword.

First Sen.   Set but thy foot
Against our rampir'd gates, and they shall ope:
So thou wilt send thy gentle heart before,
To say thou 'lt enter friendly.

Sec. Sen.   Throw thy glove,
Or any token of thine honour else, 50
That thou wilt use the wars as thy redress,
And not as our confusion; all thy powers
Shall make their harbour in our town, till we
Have seal'd thy full desire.

Alc.   Then there 's my glove,
Descend, and open your uncharged ports:
Those enemies of Timon's, and mine own,
Whom you yourselves shall set out for reproof,
Fall, and no more: and, to atone your fears
With my more noble meaning, not a man
Shall pass his quarter, or offend the stream 60

Of regular justice in your city's bounds,
But shall be render'd to your public laws
At heaviest answer.

Both.   'Tis most nobly spoken.

Alc. Descend, and keep your words.

The Senators descend, and open the gates
Enter a Messenger

Mes. My noble general, Timon is dead,
Entomb'd upon the very hem o' the sea,
And on his grave-stone this insculpture, which
With wax I brought away; whose soft impression
Interprets for my poor ignorance.

Alc. (reads)
'Here lies a wretched corse, of wretched soul bereft, †
    Seek not my name: a plague consume you, wicked 71
    caitiffs left!'
'Here lie I, Timon; who, alive, all living men did hate,
    Pass by, and curse thy fill, but pass and stay not here
    thy gait.'
These well express in thee thy latter spirits:
Though thou abhorr'dst in us our human griefs,
Scorn'dst our brain's flow, and those our droplets,
    which
From niggard nature fall; yet rich conceit
Taught thee to make vast Neptune weep for aye

On thy low grave, on faults forgiven.   Dead
Is noble Timon, of whose memory   80
Hereafter more.   Bring me into your city,
And I will use the olive, with my sword :
Make war breed peace ; make peace stint war ; make each
Prescribe to other, as each other's leech.
Let our drums strike.   *Exeunt*

Notes

THE text of *Timon* is clearly extremely corrupt, and has been the happy hunting ground of the emenders. To give the emendations proposed at all in full would extend the notes to a quite disproportionate length. I have contented myself therefore with including in the text a small number of the more generally accepted emendations, and commenting on a certain number of other dubious passages in the notes. There remain therefore a large number of passages which are certainly difficult and probably corrupt, but of which the cure is so uncertain that it seems better left to the taste of the individual reader. The more one studies the play the more one comes to feel that many passages are not so much 'corrupt' in the ordinary sense, as simply unfinished rough drafts that were to have been worked over. And if that is so, emendation is idle.

I. i. 49. *wide sea of wax.* Many conjectures, none of them carrying much conviction ('vice,' 'tax,' 'man,' 'wast').

I. i. 89. *sit;* so F. The required sense is clear, 'slip' or 'sink,' which have both been suggested, but neither is graphically easy.

I. i. 131-33. The reading given is that of F. There has been much conjecture. Some sort of sense is produced by taking *Timon* as vocative, so that the old Athenian means that the man is honest, but that is all he will be. I suspect the corruption, if any, to lie in *Timon.*

I. i. 234. *no angry wit.* An unsolved crux Just possibly *That I had no angry wit to be angry with a lord.*

I. ii. 50. *notes*; F. *noates.* If the reading is to be retained, 'notes' must be something seen, not heard, *i.e.* must be used in the sense of the Latin *notæ*; but this is not satisfactory.

I. ii. 130. *Like madness . . .*; *i.e.* 'the glory of this life is *as much* madness as this pomp is when compared to . . .'

I. ii. 244. *in paper.* The explanation 'in paper securities' is unsatisfactory, and there is probably corruption.

II. i. 10. *able.* Vaguely feeble, and probably corrupt: many conjectures. [But *cf.* 2 *Henry IV*, I. i. 43.]

II. ii. 163. *wasteful cock.* The conjecturers have had a field day over these two words; Pope shut his eyes and said firmly 'lonely room,' others, less heroic, said 'wasteful nook,' 'wakeful couch,' and 'wakeful cot'; another 'wakeful cock,' though why the cock should be wakeful, or why Flavius should go to him to pour out his sorrows is not explained; another 'wasteful cock-loft,' though why Flavius should go to the cock-loft and why it is wasteful is not explained. The only sane hope seems to be to keep as close as may be to the text and assume that Flavius is saying that he wept in the same way as the wasteful cocks were weeping spilth of wine. If there is corruption I would sooner look for it in 'retir'd': the sense needed is 'made myself like.'

III. i. 47. *And we alive that liv'd*; *i.e.* 'in so short a time'; this at least is the accepted explanation, though I cannot feel it wholly adequate.

III. ii. 11, 23, 36, 38. *so many,* and *fifty five hundred.* All very obscure: even if the second stranger did not know the sum, it is odd that Servilius should use so vague a term when Flaminius in the preceding scene has been precise: and *fifty five hundred talents* is too extravagant to be even ' humorous hyperbole,' apart from not being a round sum. We might do something with it by reading ' *five-fifty-a hundred-talents.*' But much conjecture has done little but darken counsel.

III. iii. 12. *Thrive*. Not satisfactory: but the many conjectures (*Three, Tried, Shriv'd, Thrice,* etc.) are little more so.

III. iv. 112. *Sempronius: all:* F reads Sempronius Vllorxa: *All.* One of the most famous Shakespearean cruxes, but luckily also one of the least important. Is *Vllorxa* perhaps a misreading of *Villains,* written above *rascals* in the next line as a correction, misread and transferred to the line above ?

III. v. 22. *behoove*; thus F. Usually emended to *behave.*

IV. iii. 185. *who all . . .*; *the* should probably be *thy*; and thus the emendation either of *who* to *whom,* or of *do* to *doth,* will give sense.

V. i. 149. *fall*; so F. We should perhaps read *fail* or *fault.*

V. iii. 3-4. *Timon is dead,* etc. There are two schools of commentators, (*a*) those who take this line and the next as Timon's epitaph, (*b*) those who take them to be a comment of the soldier. (*a*) are in difficulties to explain first where the inscription is, since it is apparently not on the tomb, and second why the soldier can read this and not the inscription on the tomb; (*b*) are in difficulties to explain what the second line means, and should also be troubled by the intrusive couplet. The scene is hardly important enough to worry about, but I suggest that most of the difficulties would be met by supposing that we have here two different versions of the scene of which the first was not adequately cancelled. In the first the soldier could read, and the couplet was Timon's epitaph, appropriate enough ; and the scene was to have consisted of lines 1-4, together with an announcement by the soldier that he would carry the news to his captain. In the second version the soldier could not read, and lines 3 and 4 were to be omitted altogether. Timon's epitaph does not then come till the last scene.

V. iii. 70. Here again it is hard to believe that all four lines were intended to stand. Either of the two couplets could stand by itself.

Glossary

MANY words and phrases in Shakespeare require glossing, not because they are in themselves unfamiliar, but for the opposite reason, that Shakespeare uses in their Elizabethan and unfamiliar sense a large number of words which seem so familiar that there is no incentive to look for them in the glossary. It is hoped that a glossary arranged as below will make it easy to see at a glance what words and phrases in any particular scene require elucidation. A number of phrases are glossed by what seems to be, in their context, the modern equivalent rather than by lexicographical glosses on the words which compose them.

Act First

SCENE I

line
10 BREATH'D, trained
12 PASSES, surpasses
15 TOUCH THE ESTIMATE, rise to the price
19 WATER, (as in ' diamond of the first water ')
28 UPON THE HEELS OF MY PRESENTMENT, as soon as I have presented it to Timon (as a potential patron)
39 ARTIFICIAL STRIFE, art competing with nature
43 MOE, more (the regular Eliz. form for the plural)
59 PROPERTIES, appropriates
   HIS LOVE AND TENDANCE, love and attend on him

line
60 GLASS-FAC'D, reflecting as a mirror
74 TO SCOPE, appositely
92 MORAL, allegorical
101 PERIODS, puts the full stop to
130 HER RESORT, resorting to her
136 PRECEDENT, once-experienced
171 UNCLEW, exhaust resources; (met. from unwinding a ball of wool)
176 WELL MOCK'D, clever flattery !
208 APPREHENSION, interpretation
248 ACHES, disyllable
273 OPPOSITE, antagonistic

SCENE II

line

32 APPERIL, peril

52 IN HEART, 'prosit!'

71 DICH, *contr. of* do it you

111 MUCH! *ironical*

131 SHOWS TO, appears in comparison with

137-138 THAT BEARS . . . GIFT; that has not once been rejected by his friends

151 IDLE, trifling

161 FOR HIS MIND, as a result of what he has been minded to do

line

168 ADVANCE, raise in dignity

183 PRESENTS, ? those who bring them (*cf.* l. 189)

199 LAND'S PUT TO THEIR BOOKS, is (as it were) mortgaged

203 SUCH, *sc.* friends

216 TELL, reckon

CALL TO, call on

233 COIL, ado

234 BECKS, bows

Act Second

SCENE I

22 FRACTED, dishonoured | 30 HIS, its

SCENE II

8 ROUND, blunt

112 STONES, testicles

211 FRACTIONS, disjointed remarks

Act Third

SCENE I

44 SOLIDARES, small coins (*denomination uncertain*)

SCENE IV

42 IN A CLOUD, moodily

SCENE V

line

21 UNNOTED, undemonstrative
22 BEHOOVE, ? control
24 UNDERGO, undertake
STRICT, strained
54 GUST, outburst (*or* ? relish)
55 BY MERCY, in the eyes of a
merciful judge

line

61 A SUFFICIENT BRIBER FOR, sufficient to purchase
73 HIS DRINK DANGEROUS, he is
dangerous in drink
102 TO SWELL OUR SPIRIT, to work
ourselves into higher passion
104 PRESENTLY, immediately
105 LAY FOR, plan to win

SCENE VI

4 TIRING, feeding (*met. from*
falconry)

99 MINUTE-JACKS, ? figures on a
clock, *i.e.* time servers

Act Fourth

SCENE I

12 PILL, pillage
14 LIN'D, padded

18 MYSTERIES, occupations (métiers)
25 LIBERTY, licence

SCENE III

5 IS DIVIDANT, distinguish them
12 LARDS, fattens
ROTHER, OX
16 GRISE, step
18 OBLIQUY, obliquity
27 VOTARIST, gold-worshipper
38 WAPPER'D, worn out (see
N.E.D.)
85 SALT, salacious
87 TUB-FAST, sweating-cure

116 WINDOW-BARS, lattice-work in
front of bodice
122 OBJECTS, objects calculated to
excite pity
135 OATHABLE, fit to take oath
155 QUILLETS, quibbles (*quidlibet*)
FLAMEN, priest
160 FROM, irrespective of
184 HYPERION, the sun-god
222 CHAMBERLAIN, valet

Act I. Sc. iii—continued

line		line	
224	PAGE THY HEELS, follow like pages	400	ORT, fragment
226	CAUDLE, give a pick-me-up	420	MAST, acorns (*as food for pigs*)
252	SWATH, swaddling-clothes		HEPS, hips (berries)
340	GERMAN, kin	426	CON THANKS, be grateful to
390	TOUCH, touchstone	455	MYSTERY, *see* IV. i. 18
		494	COMFORTABLE, consoling

Act Fifth

SCENE I

96	COG, cheat	181	WHITTLE, clasp-knife
97	PATCHERY, trickery	206	CLOSE, enclosure
140	IN, with regard to	218	HIS, its
150	RENDER, surrender *or* rendering of account	229	DEAR, extreme

SCENE IV

5	SCOPE, bounds	55	UNCHARGED PORTS, unassailed gates
7	TRAVERS'D, folded		
8	FLUSH, ripe	58	ATONE, calm
12	PURSY, short-winded	60	PASS HIS QUARTER, break the 'quarter' that has been given
25	TROPHIES, monuments		
	SCHOOLS, *i.e. of philosophy*		
36	SQUARE, fair	77	RICH CONCEIT, fertile imagination
47	RAMPIR'D, fortified		